GRAVITY'S GRACE

Gravity's Grace

A Memoir of End-of-Life Caregiving

Jana Branch

Labyrinth Ink

Labyrinth Ink
First Printing 2024

Library of Congress Control Number: 2024910456

ISBN 979-8-218-42247-9

Printed in USA

For more information: www.labyrinth.ink

Dedication

for anyone who comes in good faith and
finds something useful here

Epigraph

The logic of care starts out from the fleshiness and fragility of life.
Annemarie Mol

If there is a feeling that something has been lost, it may be because much has not yet been used, much is still to be found and begun.
Muriel Rukeyser

The real world is not a division between us and them, but a trap or enigma in which we are all ensnared.
Reza Negarestani

Contents

Note to the Reader

Dozens of people passed through these events. I can't tell their stories. They will be invisible or anonymous here, because this (like all tellings) is only ever partial. A few show up by name. No disrespect is meant to the many others.

No part of this is intended as medical advice.

Return

1

Dad called me back to Montana. Mom's not doing so well and, though he won't say it, neither is he. A flight from Los Angeles to Missoula, a drive up the Bitterroot Valley, and three miles up the western slope to their small ranch. I spent adolescence here, doing my best but never fitting in as a farm kid, never quite finding my place in a landscape that didn't seem to want me. At 17, I was happy to go.

Now I'm back in the living room with its low 1960s popcorn ceiling—so low that but for two inches this room would be classified as a crawlspace. The house was never the priority.

In 1972, Dad had retired from a career in the US Air Force and gone in search of a new beginning, wife and four kids in tow. The plan was to settle in Missoula, near the university where he'd get a forestry degree. Mom and Dad went house hunting, soon casting out beyond the city limits and then smaller towns farther away, until they saw this place forty miles south.

It was July and a wet year, making the ground springy underfoot. Dad says that when he walked out to the pasture and saw a motley herd of cattle including a Jersey milk cow, it felt like home, which meant it reminded him of the Wisconsin farm where he spent his childhood. Mom said little but cosigned the papers and produced the down payment from a stash she'd accumulated through frugal housekeeping over years. Relatives and friends wondered how this city girl would fare as a farm wife.

Now, he waves me toward the door. "Take your mother for a walk."

2

Mom's and my relationship is strained though better than it was. Other than our history, we don't have much in common. I haven't provided kids and grandkids to gossip about, so we talk about variations on the weather.

Now we walk, chatting pleasantries, an ordinary act that still requires effort. We go slowly, to accommodate her ankle and knee, not so sturdy since a fall down school stairs in one of her last years as a first-grade teacher.

I ask how she is. What's keeping her busy? Her answers are short. Vague. She comments on my rental car in the driveway. She asks how my work is going. I say it's fine. Freelance work is always feast or famine, but I get along. She nods.

Then: "And where did you grow up? Do you have brothers and sisters?"

3

I had often felt like a stranger to my mother, but now I *am* a stranger. She makes expert small talk with me, the kind that could keep me chatting so I never quite notice that this genteel lady is, under the polite patter, struggling to make sense of who I am and where she is.

We walk across the yard to the back door of the house where she's lived for fifty years, but is it hers? She thinks she may be told to leave soon.

Back in the house, Dad can tell that I've seen what he wanted me to see. Do I imagine that he looks relieved? We don't talk much, but we *can* talk. He appreciates how I think things through, exploring possibilities, weighing pros and cons.

He's been managing the household, over time taking on each task that Mom has dropped—driving, shopping, laundry, cooking, paying bills—along with his usual outdoor chores and projects. He shepherds her through the day's routine, from morning juice and coffee to reminding her which side of the bed is hers. When they both have insomnia, they sit at the kitchen table together reading poems ingrained from their childhoods. "I wandered lonely as a cloud." "Barefoot Boy." "Invictus." He works it all around (as he puts it) "how Mom is now." In their late 80s, this is a lot. Too much, in fact.

They've been getting by with remote help and every-some-months visits from the siblings, all older, who drive or fly in from the next state or across the country. For years, that's been enough. Now something more is needed.

4
=====

Dad announces that we're going to the grocery store. He suggests I drive and keep Mom company while he does the shopping. But first, he'd like me to get Mom ready.

In better times, she always dressed with care and unassuming style, short blonde hair carefully curled, glasses properly clean, and no makeup save for pink lipstick. She didn't dress to stand out but nevertheless had an air of quiet elegance. Today, she's put on a comfortable but lifeless stained sweatshirt and worn pants. Her gray hair, hanging limp, is long overdue for a cut, but she doesn't want to go to a salon and doesn't allow this stranger to do anything more than hand her a comb. We do find a clean sweatshirt and wipe the fingerprints from her glasses.

On behalf of her former self, I feel a sting of sad embarrassment, but Dad's not bothered. Over the years, standards have relaxed by degrees. It is what it is.

In the parking lot, Dad points at the corral of shopping carts. I fetch one, and they each hold a side of the handle to steady themselves walking to the entrance. I watch for tall pickup trucks backing out, heart feeling a new fracture. In public, their vulnerability is more stark.

In the store, Dad usually leaves Mom on a chair by the pharmacy while he shops. Does she sit waiting? If she wanders, I'm guessing that one of the regular clerks would help her. This is an aging valley, and some of the cashiers have been around for years. They can see when a little help goes a long way, especially for folks too proud to ask for it themselves.

Today, Mom and I walk through a few aisles while Dad goes ahead with the cart. She's fascinated by the colorful packages, the ones purposely stocked on low shelves to grab kids' attention. We catch up with Dad by the toilet paper. He can't read the package to see if it's septic safe. I find the words and show him. He nods and points to the biggest pack.

At the checkout, that sting of embarrassment returns. I begin to suspect it's less about her than about me. Am I worried that people will see her on my arm and think I haven't done enough to care for her? *Who would let their mother out of the house looking like that?* I don't want her to appear diminished, and I don't want to seem indifferent.

I feel a stern internal urge that we should be doing better to keep up appearances. An old lesson with no clear origin but tied to her inexorably. Embarrassment at our unadorned selves being seen, our least attractive (possibly broken) parts on display. *We'll be judged and found wanting.*

I walk beside her, but I am not my mother. I am, in meaningful ways, not even her daughter anymore. The dimensions of her deterioration shadow me, but this isn't about me. I'm not the keeper of her story. I can guide its possibilities, but she's the one living it. An insight that will bear repeating to myself: *What's happening isn't about me.*

5

She gifted me with first with life, then with a habit for sweet things, nibbled or gobbled in secret. Starting at six, we did it together. As I got older, we fell into separate patterns. I knew where she hid her cookies, Twinkies, and ice cream. I knew where her box of Ayds Reducing Plan Candy was, too, and occasionally ate some myself. I had my own secrets, though she knew I was buying Three Musketeers bars and sneaking Space Food Sticks after school. We'd bake cookies, and some-times she'd declare that after this we'd go on a diet together: *no more cookies.* Fat chance. Dark moods that came down from her father's side of the family pressed on us both, a private weather, storm and fog.

At nine, I stood on a hot summer sidewalk in front of our house and felt my bulging belly. I imagined unzipping my skin from neck to crotch, able to step out of the jiggling, squishy fat suit. Or severing my head from my body. Everything below my neck would stay at home. At school, my head would float through the hallway and rest on my desk. (School mostly worked. Everything else felt wrong.)

By twenty, I'd bashed my way through college and into a job, every day diced into solitary food rituals, binges flipping into anorexia then bulimia. The shame and self destruction rolled on, though no one saw through top grades and my relentless work ethic. Mom was so proud.

Meanwhile, I passed people on the street who seemed buoyant, relaxed, at home with other people and themselves. *Why can't I be like that?* I wondered. *What would it take to be like that?*

On the pretext of dream analysis, I found talk therapy. After a couple of years, food felt less tyrannical. Life became cautiously livable. One day I described an unfamiliar bubbling inside. The therapist suggested I might be feeling happy.

I went home for a visit. We sat at the kitchen table, and I said the quiet part out loud: The obsessive thoughts about food—the secretive what, when, where, and how—*aren't* fate. The dark moods *aren't* destiny. *It's possible to feel so much better.*

Mom's peaches-and-cream complexion drained to white, careful smile frozen in a thin line. Too late, I saw it through her eyes: I had brought the unruly thing we never admitted into the room. I'd spoken the monster out of its box. Our silent bond, the feeling that *it can't be so terrible if we do it together,* was suddenly gone. My life-altering change was, on its flipside, a rejection of what we'd shared. A rejection of *her.* And speaking of it threatened the carefully balanced way of being she'd constructed over years.

"Why?" she wanted to know.

Because the way I felt all those years was unbearable. Unbearable.

With love in her eyes, she pleaded, "I want the *old* Jana back."

The suicidal one?

She pursed her lips, not protesting.

I talked to Dad. He agreed I had a point, then shrugged. Loyalty came first. The family rallied around her. With that support, the mood swings and sugar binges would always work for her, by turns torment and relief.

But I couldn't retreat back into that suffering, and I couldn't endorse hers. For years we didn't speak. And once we patched things up, albeit raggedly, we never spoke about it again.

Decades later, I count that passage as a dark and profound gift. She led me into a maze where a tacit plea echoed: *find the way outta here.* It took years to carve out the perspective and skills that freed me enough to come back to this place where she's still trapped, now with a sideswipe of dementia.

6

The decision I face has less to do with family history and everything to do with entanglement that began with DNA's collision and an umbilical cord. The imperative of mutual care—a moral demand—erupts from somewhere beyond rational thought. Decades ago, she cared for this family on days when I'm sure she'd had enough of us. She stuck with us, even if her memories of those years are mostly gone. It feels like time for me to stick with her.

The lingering hope that Mom and I might find mutual forgiveness is gone. That work is now mine to do, as I've suspected it always has been. Unexpectedly, the years of estrangement fade to irrelevance, and a new possibility takes shape.

Dad won't ask me to move back to Montana (he'd never presume) but hints at how good it would be to have one of us kids nearby. He's asked me to come home to see, and I can't not see what's right in front of me. Mom's in need of care, both the woman disappearing and one emerging who has different demands.

Dad needs care, too. Presence. Someone nearby. Among us four kids, I'm the only one in a position to do it.

7

I make the unlikeliest of plans—to move back to Montana. I don't ask. I don't want to talk about reasons I can barely articulate myself.

A certainty has settled in while adrenalin washes through, water over a stream bed. *Can I help them on their terms while also hanging on to myself? Will I become a moth battering at the window, frustrated, getting nowhere, but nonetheless content in the exertion?*

I return, improbably, remembering that the one who returns is not the same one who went. I hold a horizon in mind that isn't limited by geology or family history. I know the way out, and that will enable me to stay.

Wander

8

At first, I stop in as a neighbor would, a friendly face who helps with errands and chores. I've rented an apartment a mile up the road. Dad and I agree that moving back into the house would distress Mom and feed increasingly frequent delusions that she lives in a boarding house.

I visit a few mornings a week. Dad soon asks me to stop by more often, then every day, then earlier each morning. He and I sit at the table over coffee and donut holes while Mom rustles around upstairs. He likes me to be around when she first comes downstairs, to help her in ways that are uncomfortable for him.

Today she's forgotten to put on pants. I go upstairs and find a pair that matches her top. She holds onto the back of her chair while I ask her to lift one leg and then the other to get her into them. She and Dad joke about how nice it is for her to have a personal dresser.

She still senses when she's lost another thread, even though she can't put her finger on what's gone missing. She'll forget about the lack of pants, but remnants of distress could stick and disrupt her mood. So we stay calm and cheery to guard against the stuff that could stick.

The brain is failing. Some long-held memories still circulate, but nothing new has a place to land. No new memories. Routines crumbling. The arrow of time collapsing.

I smile hard. My uncle, whose wife has Alzheimer's, calls it *pumping sunshine.* I smile while stooping under the sadness. I know from experience that such contortions can, over time, become fixed. I, too, guard against feelings that could stick.

9

By dumb luck, I've rented the caretaker's apartment on a property that has a labyrinth, 108 feet across, its circuits marked by fieldstones and surrounded by crabapple, blue spruce, chokecherry, oak, and other trees; rose bushes; Concord grape vines; hops that trail to the sky; and hundreds of lavender plants proliferated over twenty years. The owner, Helmut, is a family friend. His wife Patty inspired it, and together they built it and opened it to people in search of walking meditation. She and Mom taught at the same elementary school across the valley and commuted back and forth together through all weather. Patty died a few years ago.

It's a mile up the hill but a universe away from the architecture of my family. Walking the labyrinth will be a solace, especially on days of alien surprise, when another remnant of my mother disappears and someone new appears. The necessity that brought me to Montana propels me here, too, winding to the center and back again.

A maze and labyrinth are often confused for one another, but they're entirely different experiences. A maze is a puzzle of blind alleys and dead ends until, by some luck or will or canny problem solving, the walker finds their way to the center. But this is no triumph. Getting back out is a problem of its own.

A labyrinth is a single path that requires one decision—to enter. Then simply follow the path. It takes me tantalizingly close to the center after only a few turns. But before reaching the center, that path must wind back on itself, reach the outer edges while wandering through 360 degrees and only then arrive at the center, the still point around which everything else revolves.

Today, I choose to enter.

10

Every morning, I drive over the wooden cattle guard into my parents'
place, a modest-sized ranch big enough to keep a couple dozen cows
and calves and grow some hay. I leave most of myself at that threshold.
My interests narrow to what's needed here.

A round of chores takes shape from the end of spring through
summer. On hot days, I dip a bucket into the irrigation ditch and haul
up water to pour over the rhubarb. Some of the stalks are big enough
to pull, but I'll leave them unless I have time to bake.

I visit the barn cat, pet her until she drops into the corral dust and
gets so busy rolling in it that she doesn't follow when I leave. Robins
fight over territory. In the upper field, a quail hen lays eggs under dried
leaves that match her mottled gray and brown feathers so well she and
her nest disappear.

Every day I eat lunch with my parents, like I did when I was a kid,
except that now I do the cooking. I still set the table. Mom still does
the dishes (usually), the last kitchen task she remembers how to do,
though bowls and plates end up in unusual spots in the cupboards. We
eat off the dishes Dad brought back from Japan in 1969. She marvels at
the design: "I've seen this pattern a lot. It must be so popular! It's in our
real house, too."

11

Spring brush piles have been burned, long days turning coals over with a pitchfork, encouraging flames on hunks of cottonwood. Some took two days of smolder before slumping to ash. Heat bent a cloche of air over what remained. After dark, a slight wind fanned embers to orange that winked and faded.

The ash would fit in a six-gallon bucket if I collected it. But I won't. Wind will scatter it or, as the Red Angus heifers and young bull walk over it, become part of the soil. Eventually, the burned circle will disappear under a humid stand of green grass stalks and leaves.

So much unwieldy material. So little left behind. Proof of how improbable physical form is to begin with, molecules bonded around oceans of air. It took a tractor to move the fallen trees. Now, they're powder.

12

I drive north to Missoula to meet a wise friend for an hour's conversation. He's passing through on the interstate, back home to the west coast after an endurance bike ride, 42 hours on gravel roads, no sleep through day and night. A space of hallucination, transformation, and deep meditation via intense activity. He calls it "crossing the Rubicon."

His mom had dementia. He went through it with her, his father at his side, and he knows how it goes. He sees better than I do what's ahead. He's sure I can do it. I hear that more as hope than prediction.

He lets me talk, winding around to things I can only look at sidelong, things that seem strange to everyone but one who's been through it before. The visit is kind and deep, and it makes me aware of how daunting, open-ended, uncontrollable, sad, and necessary the task is that I've taken on.

His quiet intensity, all vertical stability and force, is like sitting near a warm, steady flame. By contrast, I've damped myself down into a smolder meant to burn long rather than hot. I'm not sure it's the best way forward. Right now, it is what it is.

I listen to the intimacy of his knowledge, the strength of his care. He talks about the deep disorientation that circulates around the person with dementia as well as those who care for that person. The ground you thought was stable is quicksand.

One part of me leans toward what he says. Another part steps back so as not to learn too much. Some things will only be borne with a dose of ignorance.

I drive home to the south, up the valley—"up" because I drive against the river's flow, which runs north. The logic of two-dimensional maps doesn't apply here. The compass rose is no match for gravity's meandering.

I pass a historical marker on the highway. This valley was built on forced displacements and successive waves of hope and failure. I'm passing through, moved by a crosshatch of choice and circumstance. This place won't shrug even a millimeter when I'm gone. There is no way to succeed at what I'm doing. The task is impossible and necessary.

I know well the breadth of sky, the rounded profile of the Sapphire Mountains to the east and the taller, jagged outline of the Bitterroot Mountains to the west. I'm still gobsmacked. The landscape presses in, demanding that I declare, as Dad insists no matter what the weather, "Nice day..." and sometimes adds, "...considering the alternative."

My head is pounding. How can this bright summer day feel so much like a narrow tunnel with no light? As dark as being inside a skull, its gray stuff shrinking as structures fall apart. My mother has dementia, and no one who's paying attention escapes the horror of losing this basic premise: *I know who I am.*

13

My job now is to be ready for whatever comes next. Flexibility, curiosity, and willingness to adapt will be crucial. I can't afford to let stress make me brittle.

I need to guard against too much knowingness. I'm usually the one in the know, but here I know so little. False confidence is dangerous, crowding out humility and seeding a sense of control grounded on air. That's as true for helping around the ranch as helping Mom.

With one eye on all that, I read up on dementia. I comb websites. I watch videos about the stages of progression and typical behaviors and feel the collective shrug where information ends and medical mystery begins.

I avoid the rubbernecking resources. So much is some version of *can you believe what she/he did now?! It's crazy!*

It's not crazy. It's dementia.

14

An immediate problem: How to respond to repetition. Mom will ask the same question over and over (and over) again. Nothing seems to quiet her need to know, because she can't make a new memory. She can't durably connect her question with Dad's answer.

After a dozen go-rounds, he loses patience, gets up out of his chair at the head of the kitchen table, and goes outside. He doesn't know it, but taking a break is one of the recommendations for caregivers nearing the end of their rope.

The other option I try is redirection. Change the subject. Start a new activity. It sometimes helps. Other times she turns away, suspicious.

Mom's deteriorating inner world is uncharted territory. I don't—can't—know what she's going through. And as I try to help her out of a looping question with no exit, I quell my own rising impatience by reminding myself that her ever-diminishing self still deserves respect. Dad and I manage these moments, but we don't manage her.

15

Mom spends long hours "wool gathering" (as she puts it), patching outward clues together with vanishing scraps in her mind. She worries, which isn't new for her, but now her worries have to do with questions anyone would have in a foreign place. What can she do here? Is she safe? Can she stay? Are we here to help or hurt her? Or is her mind playing tricks on her?

Giving her a choice has become a small terror. Red or blue? She suspects there's only one right answer but has no idea how to get to it. Her brow knits. Her hand, restless, rubs the arm of her rocking chair. It's becoming kinder to guide her to one answer, based on her taste expressed over decades.

She can't remember that she's been diagnosed with dementia. That's not a factor in her puzzling as she gazes out the living room window, lamenting the small blonde circle she can see on the trunk of a Ponderosa pine across the road. Months ago, a county road crew trimmed a low-hanging limb and left that scar. It offends her.

Her disorientation sometimes echoes something I recognize from her past. I watch for clues in behavior and feeling as much as in words. *Who is she becoming? Who does she believe herself to be? What bothers her now? What gives her pleasure?* And practical questions: *What's changed since yesterday? What does that mean for how she feels and what she needs?*

There is no cure. No surgery. No heroic medical intervention. General advice must be adapted to her particularity. (We are all particular, if sometimes predictable, in our deterioration.)

16

Dad has just come back into the house after his usual morning talk down by the barn with Les, the rancher who keeps his cattle on the place. Les is a man of few words, walks with a slight hitch, and is always trailed by his smiling cow dog Sammy. He was raised riding horses and working cattle with family in the northern Montana that Ivan Doig writes about. But stories other people write about places we know in our bones rarely reflect our truth.

From a one-room country schoolhouse to college to a career at the mill, raising a family, Les' stoic heart bears more than I can imagine. He can handle animals, manage a ranch, build houses, and fix just about any farm machinery that breaks. Dad admires his background, range of skills, and work ethic.

Dad and Les have the same thorough eye for maintenance and repair. They both care about square joints, accuracy that's both practical in its performance and pleasing to the eye. They'd never say there's grace in that combination, but I see it in the way they work. Never precious, but never without care.

Mom watches them from the window over the kitchen sink. She says she misses having a friend like that of her own.

17

Dad sold his herd of White Park cattle just as Les was looking for pasture to rent. Their deal was done on a handshake, and seven years later it holds. Dad sees how well Les cares for his herd of Red Angus and gets to see the agricultural cycle play out, even though he's no longer doing much of the work. Les sees how much it means to Dad to keep the land productive. They both harrow fields in spring and mow hay in summer, but Dad no longer works cattle. Too dangerous without fast reflexes and steady feet, he says.

I was never a natural at ranch life, but being here means I'm now an extra body on the odd day when one is needed. Les keeps things low-key by knowing his cows' paths of least resistance and using more carrot than stick. I see his close attention and patience. He moves close to the animals' pace rather than the on-the-clock-get-it-done rush I'm used to. He lets the cows' inclinations and intelligence play out while staying a step ahead of calves that dash away in any direction but the one that would take them back to the herd. I help him bring cows into the corral. When I miscalculate and a few split off to gallop down the pasture, Les just sighs a little. We try again.

When Dad takes the tractor out, I walk along to open and close gates, so Dad can drive through without climbing down from the seat, then heaving himself back up on the tall step that he jokes gets taller every year. I learn to use the chainsaw to cut logs for firewood. After some rough going, Dad generously tells me not to worry. "It all burns just the same."

I'm not good at any of it, but it's good enough. Body and mind fall into a rhythm that bends with the season. I don't know it now, but the steadiness I cultivate to safely do ranch work will serve me well navigating the care Mom and Dad will need.

18

The short-focus, skittery style of attention that helped me dodge and weave through five-lane traffic around Los Angeles doesn't serve me here. I need to slow down, look not just ahead and behind, left and right, but in all directions through all degrees.

This is, I realize, how my eyes travel as I walk the labyrinth. Linear gives way to circular. Constant gives way to cyclical. Appropriate speed becomes a matter of season, weather, growth, and rest. Dad's winter driving advice for slippery roads will be apt: It's not how fast you can go but how fast you can stop.

19

Les is on the edge of a hayfield looking at the short grass. He leans on a shovel. He's been there for awhile. Doesn't seem like he's doing much.

In fact, he's watching rivulets of water run across in small channels he's dug. He looks closely, up and across the field, beyond and back. He sees how and where the water's running and considers what needs doing to get it where it'll do the most good.

His thought isn't visible, but it will show up in the health of the grass and quantity of hay he'll raise off this patch. Even Dad will admit that Les does a better job of irrigating these irregular fields than he ever did.

Attention is everything here, and there's no value in rushing it. Like finding the right tempo for a song that allows the listener to really hear the music, there's a tempo that fits here. It allows for the human-scale endeavor to play out.

20

I wonder what courage it takes for Mom to wake up each morning into a place she doesn't recognize as her own, look at clothes she doesn't understand, gamely put on what draws her eye, then walk slowly down the stairs to whatever and whoever awaits. A man she may or may not know. A routine that's no longer her own. Goings-on that erupt without her say-so. Noises she can no longer tolerate, like the chugging metal box that sloshes water, goes silent, then sloshes again in an uncertain rhythm that unnerves her.

She sits as still as she can most of the day. Fewer movements, fewer mistakes?

21

I play a lot of *what if...*

What if one of them dies in their sleep? What do I do? Who do I call? I assume that in the moment I won't think clearly, and it will help to have a plan. I research. Ask around. Make notes.

What if an ambulance needs to come to the house? During the snowy months, I'll shovel more of the driveway clear than Dad expects. He's not thinking of how much space an ambulance needs or how fast a gurney could be wheeled to the front door, but I am.

Lying awake at night, it's a way of pushing that glib throwaway—*we'll all die sometime*—to a more practical, immediate reality: My parents will die. And because I'm here, the surrounding circumstances will be, to some extent, in my hands.

How can I do the best for them? They'd say they have a good life. How, when it's time, can I help them have a good death? So much of that comes down to details and proximity, being within arm's reach to make time-sensitive decisions. There's no substitute for presence, and there are no shortcuts to preserving dignity, ensuring comfort, and creating ground for whatever good is possible to the last breath.

22

Mom sits hunched by the phone, looking cold. Dad brings her a quilted jacket and struggles to help her put it on. She doesn't want it.

She says she's not cold. But she's behaving like she's cold. Her posture says she's cold. Has the dementia severed her conscious recognition of that basic bodily sense? Or is she like a kid lost in whatever she's doing, so fully in another projected place that the reality of the body is irrelevant? How many times, as a mother and teacher, did she lovingly scold kids to put on a sweater or coat?

Later, when she throws the jacket off, is it because she's too warm? Or does the texture suddenly bother her? Or the color? I invite her to sit at the table, next to the wood stove. Her desires are so few, and I try to respect them.

She no longer files her nails, and they're starting to break. She allows me to give her a manicure and enjoys it so much she takes a $20 bill out of a drawer to pay me. I take it, thank her, and later slip it to Dad.

She admires her nails then says with a note of frustration, "I don't know what I need anymore." She refuses my offer of a pedicure, but when I stand by the door ready to leave for the day, she comes to me with her socks off, gnarly nails on display.

"Can we do a pedicure tomorrow?" I ask. She nods.

23

Sometimes she can identify people in photos. Mostly not.

On the phone, her conversational patter of open-ended questions keeps the focus off of her. Most people she talks to are happy to talk about themselves, so this works out.

How are you? I'm fine. How's the family? Oh, that's nice. How's work? Oh, that's good. Where are you? What are you doing for fun? Alright then, take care. Love you. Love you back.

Dad always tells her who's on the phone, so as she takes the receiver she knows a name—which is different from knowing the person.

24

Lady, a rescue border collie, is among the beloved beings swallowed by Mom's dementia. In her mid-teens, Lady is largely deaf and mostly blind but has a keen sense of duty and still makes her way around the ranch on the strength of her nose.

Mom is her favorite person, and she sits by Mom's rocking chair, as she has for the previous decade. But instead of taking in Lady's soulful gaze, Mom looks at her with mild curiosity, little connection, and no idea of stroking her head.

25

Mom's bored. The capacity to do things that used to keep her busy is falling away. An avid reader all her life, now she reads the first sentence of a romance novel over and over. It feels good to hold a book, but the image, characters, and action in the words melt by the time she reaches the period. She stops. Goes back to the beginning. She remembers the rhythm, but there's nothing to build on. She can't make a new memory, so no story can take hold.

She no longer plays her piano. Quilting projects are shelved. Magazines go unread. The rush of images and sounds on TV are incomprehensible. She's confused or distressed by newspaper headlines. She no longer writes newsy letters to friends and family. Junk mail and personal letters are indistinguishable, so they all go into the same grocery bags to be archived in cupboards and behind the dryer.

She still fills in a few answers in the newspaper's daily crossword puzzle. She still sweeps the floor, slowly, patchily, absorbed in the motion. She wants to write a few Christmas cards, but after I address the envelopes, the cards sit untouched.

She was always artistic, so I get some colored pencils and an adult coloring book with outlines reminiscent of Scandinavian floral designs, a nod to family heritage. She's offended. "Do you think I'm a *child?*"

"Of course not," I laugh. "These days, coloring isn't just for kids. There's even an adult coloring club at the library." The look on her face is clear: *If those adults want to act like children, let them. But I won't.*

26

She asks, "I can't go to school?"

Dad pats her hand and says with the trace of a smile, "No, honey. We're old. We're out to pasture. You're not a teacher anymore. I can't do much anymore either. And what I can do, I do slowly."

Her mouth trembles. She sighs. He hugs her, and she leans into him. This, for now, is normal.

27

Summer dissolves into fall. Fall solidifies into winter. From her rocking chair, she points out the window and says, "Look at the cloud pictures!" She says over and over how bright the snow looks, sometimes observing that the snow isn't white at all but is in fact many colors. At twilight, she notes that it's blue.

Most days, she looks out at the bank of junipers punctuated with crabapple trees and marvels that there's no breeze. "Nothing's moving." And wonders if she's looking at a fake movie set or if what she sees is real life. How can we tell the difference between the real and the fake, she wants to know, when nothing's moving?

28

I am daughter. But not primarily daughter and, crucially, not only daughter. I slip among roles that help me call up whatever skills I need to meet the circumstance. Researcher. Elder advocate. Personal assistant. Project manager. Ranch hand. Cook. Housekeeper. Shopper. Accountant. Figure out what they need, get it, or do it. Question gently, offer choices, and don't argue.

I'm here to support, not control. It's a dance I learned from Great Aunt Florence. I always wondered why she chose me to attend her last weeks, through hospital, ER, and home hospice. Was it for this?

29

Time's reach forward and backward has contracted into a dot with no direction. She shimmers in an ever-present *now.* Some spiritual traditions consider this a sign of enlightenment. I'm not so sure.

Old, intense memories are dragged into this always-present, an inside-out, involuntary time travel. Her mother dies afresh, every time Mom asks and is told that Amy has been gone for forty years. She loses her father again and again. She continues to ask. They continue to die. She mourns every time. The original wound remains with no relief possible except the forgetting that will come as even those are destroyed by what's going on in her body.

What does the present become if future and past are gone? How do we even know what *now* is if it's not energized, shaped, and shadowed by what's already been and what's to come? A pure present is a form of death, as a dynamic body that reaches pure balance—homeostatis—is dead. Life is flux. *Now* is a step into a running stream.

But this is just a guess and is likely too heady. Mom may have no ability to think ahead or remember what just happened, but her memory isn't just cognitive. She can't tell me what happened ten minutes ago, but her body hangs on to feeling. I see it in her face and posture. The content may be gone, but tone and intensity still land in a part of her that defines an ongoing mood. Her internal clock has no numbers, but it has colors.

30

Is Mom getting worse, or do I just see more because I spend more time with her now? Dad likes me to have lunch with them in the hope that I can encourage Mom to eat something like a real meal. He says she's snacking a lot. Donut holes. Ice cream. Cookies. And now the treats showing up in holiday packages.

I ask if she wants lunch. *No.* I wait twenty minutes, then tell her we're sitting down and that we'd like her to join us. She comes to the table and, standing by her chair, admires the Jell-O's red jeweltone lit by a sunbeam. Dad asks her to sit down, so we can say grace. She does but then forgets about her own food. Dad puts his hand on hers, a gentle reminder. She picks up her fork but ends up feeding most of her chicken to Lady, who sits at her side. Dad, who has just told me how much he dislikes dogs that beg at the table, says nothing.

After a few minutes, Mom asks if we're the only ones eating lunch. Is there enough food for the many other people who live in the house?

31

The daily routine is prone to ghostly disruptions. She sees her mother walking in the front yard. She tells me her father is in the kitchen making lunch. Are these memories stuck somewhere out of reach but still able to heave through into dreamlike wakefulness? Or is this hallucination? Does it matter?

More to the point: Does it worry her? Is this anxiety a sign of her mind asking for some resolution or seeking comfort? We reminisce about her parents, though I doubt that any story I know explains what their specters want from or for her.

32

Late afternoon, just before Christmas, Mom's brother calls me to say that his wife has died. He asks me to deliver the news to his sister. I wonder if I should wait until morning, remembering some advice about not delivering bad news at day's end, sending people to bed with loss freshly in mind. The moon is just past full. Mom's sleep is already disturbed, and grief could provoke darker dreams.

Then another thought: Maybe she won't care. She and her sister-in-law were never close. Mom and Dad hadn't seen her for nearly fifty years. They don't even talk on the phone at holidays. Maybe this news will be non-news, greeted with a shrug: *Oh, well, we're all getting old.* This seems the likeliest reaction, so I go to the ranch.

I'm wrong. Dad helps her patch together who this newly dead person is. She stands in the kitchen looking lost, cheeks and mouth quivering, brow knitted, nearly crying but not quite. "What a summer this is! It's just one thing after the next!" she says.

We sit at the table and talk. "So many people we know..." And I see in her face the barrage of wounds that are not in the past but are happening right now, grief piled on grief. Her mother. Her father. Some parts of her memory are gone (she doesn't remember having had children, though she believes Dad when he says, "your daughter is on the phone"). But some events cling tenaciously to the present and refuse to be shed. What people call memory "loss" is also, paradoxically, a loss of the constructive ability to forget.

She says again, "What is it about this time of year?! It's just one thing after the next!" And Dad comments that, indeed, this is a time of year when a lot of people go. The darkest days, the longest nights.

And then the crux of it. She looks at Dad and asks, "*You're* fine, right?" She knows, at least in this moment, who he is to her.

"Yes," he says and raps his knuckles on the wood table.

She looks at me, pleading, "He's my rock."

She's been struck with the close reality that spouses die. *Her* spouse might die, an old fear of unspeakable magnitude that she carried for years as a military wife. Her very identity is knitted into him. He is her everything. In earlier days, she would've called it true love. I don't envy it.

33

Winter drags on. Her footing is too precarious for walks outside, but so much time indoors turns the house into a maze of boredom and frustration. She spends part of her day going through drawers and hiding things she deems precious, like rings and her toothbrush.

She stares out the window for awhile then declares, "I think we're in some sort of … prehistoric time … when it just snows all the time!"

We laugh, and Dad says, "It seems that way." We talk about the days getting longer, how the first day of spring is coming.

34

Mom asks where I'm going next. I tell her I don't have plans to go anywhere. Dad says he finds it comforting to know I'm living up the hill. But we quickly run out of things to talk about. I'm no source of local news or neighborhood gossip. Over a cup of coffee, I'm useless.

Beyond their need for some bits of help and my need to offer that help, we don't have much in common. We don't talk politics or world events. Dad sometimes lobs an opinion. I duck. I realize he mostly wants an audience. I lay down a certain amount of myself at the door, take a deep breath, sit down, and listen.

Still, I'm touched when I leave for the day and, at the door, he says something kind. "Thanks for stopping by." "Thanks for fixing the TV." "Thanks for the good lunch. We're eating better now than we have in years."

Mom stands mutely by but one day surprises me by asking me to come back tomorrow. "Don't quit us cold turkey," she says.

35

Dad has a nasty cold that seems headed for his lungs. He says the best thing he can do for her is to get better. He even agrees to see his doctor instead of toughing it out. He's not as cavalier as he used to be, relying on a history of good health and will to get through anything with an aspirin and a night's sleep.

Now, he's acutely aware that Mom's care depends in large measure on him. He's determined to outlive her, to use all his capability to see her through whatever's coming.

36

She's taken to cutting things up to make little cleaning rags. She snips apart the cloth napkins that were always too special to use. Now she's starting in on her clothes.

Dad shrugs. "They're her things. She can do what she wants with them."

He doesn't complain when she pulls all her clothes out of her dresser and piles them on their bed. He only protests when she puts them back into *his* dresser drawers. This is a bridge too far.

37

Late afternoon: Mom wants to go home. She's taken her purse from the closet and sits on the couch by the front door. She wants Dad to get the car and drive her there. Reminding her that she is, in fact, already at home gets nowhere. The home she means is the Minneapolis house of her teenage years.

She's sundowning. I've read about it, and now here it is.

Dad tries to distract her. He suggests it's too late. He doesn't want to drive in the dark. Fine, she says. She'll walk. Will he walk there with her?

After an hour or so of other distractions, she tires and goes upstairs to bed. Dad wakes in the middle of the night. She's awake, staring eerily at him. Watching him.

38

She's forgotten how clothes work. She wears a bathrobe backwards. She cheerily drapes pants legs around her neck and over her shoulders like a shawl. She puts a turtleneck shirt on inside out, saying the seams against her skin bother her. (Dementia can make the senses, including touch, more acute.)

I see her creativity—a playfulness—emerge in the space where what's customary has gone missing. By forgetting how things are supposed to work, she finds room for what she prefers.

Another day, she comes down the stairs in five shirts layered one over the next. Later, I look at a pile of clothes and try to let their forms melt into that childhood prehistory when I didn't know what they were for, like saying a word over and over and over until it suddenly crosses some boundary and becomes nonsense.

Table. Book. Jar. Pencil. I look around and try to imagine these things no longer being things I understand how to use. Just dumb objects. If I could no longer use them, would that make me useless? How much of my value is premised on being useful, able to act, move, choose, grasp, build, earn, spend, and ask?

I try to imagine the world I move in fading into an alien place where clothes and coffee machines require something I can't give. I can't get there except for a whiff of terror and a hope that someone then would be patient with me.

39

Mom has forgotten how packaging works. She stands at the kitchen counter with a half-gallon round carton of ice cream. Instead of taking the lid off, she's stabbed at its transparent window with a big metal stirring spoon until she made her way in. Now she nibbles ice cream off the very end of the spoon. The proportion makes me wonder if she did this as a little girl with a too-big spoon.

She's forgotten that she used to eat this way in secret. I follow Dad's example, letting her do as she likes. As he says, "She enjoys it more when she thinks she's getting away with something."

But she sees me see her. "That looks good," I say. She ignores me and turns back to the carton. She's having her way with what she wants, more freely than I've ever seen her do.

40

I find signposts of her decline. Instructions she wrote for making a pot of coffee are taped inside a cupboard door. The wobbly, sloping letters are midway between her trademark refined script and today's shaky fracture. This must be a note she wrote a couple of years ago.

I mention it to Les, and he recalls how, when he and Dad would sit down at the table for a talk over coffee, Dad would ask Mom to make a fresh pot. She would stand in front of the machine, fiddling with things on the counter but not getting the coffee canister out of the cupboard or filling the carafe with water or putting a new filter in the basket... until Dad's impatience got the better of him and he'd move her aside to make it himself. Les remembers Dad's uncharacteristic irritation, a sign (I imagine) that he was holding down fear about what was unfolding in front of him and he was not yet ready to see.

The first sign Dad could no longer ignore was this: Mom forgot how to drive. She stopped the car in the middle of our small Main Street. She went into the post office for help, saying the car had broken down. The manager went out, started the car, and pulled it into a parking spot before calling Dad. He picked her up and tells me the car was fine. She just forgot, in the middle of driving, how it all worked.

41

She worries about the boarders who she thinks live upstairs. Is she a boarder, too? Did someone pay the rent, or will she be evicted soon?

And she continues to sundown, with tearful insistence that we take her home, meaning the brick house where she was a teenager—and where her mother in those years rented out extra bedrooms to young women who were students at the nearby university.

After all the usual redirection fails, Dad tells her: "Honey, this home you want to go to exists only in your imagination."

42

She calls me "the girl from up the hill," and as months turn into a year, she becomes suspicious of me. She believes I'm here to steal her husband. She says that because I'm cooking, cleaning, doing laundry, and yardwork, her husband will fall in love with me. Get me pregnant. She thinks he'll run off with me, leaving her alone to fend for herself.

I hear the echo of Dear Abby relationship drama Mom and Dad have read from the daily newspaper column for decades. But aside from the absurd storyline, I hear her fear that she's become useless. I can't dismiss the heartbreaking logic: *The one who does the work is the one who gets the love.*

Has being loved always felt conditional to her? Did she wake up every day believing, in some deep part of herself, that she had to earn her place here? In spite of decades of tender proclamations and devotion from Dad, has she never been completely sure of her place in their shared life?

And is this related to the conditional shadow I felt as a kid, always working to earn my place in her affections with good grades, good behavior, and our shared secret?

Now she stands at the sink over dirty dishes she jealously declares are hers to wash. Then forgets why she's there, staring out the window across the yard to the barn. I reach around her, run warm water, and squeeze in a drizzle of dish soap. Something clicks. She picks up a gray dishrag, the one she refuses to trade for one less worn, and swirls it over a plate. Today, her place is secure.

43

Dad goes upstairs for his usual post-lunch nap. For a few hours, Mom is on her own, which is no longer safe. She forgets he's upstairs and has wandered outside looking for him. From now on, I'll stay until he's awake.

Mom is in her usual place, looking out the front picture window at the mountains. I think we might have a chat, but she gives me an icy look: "I don't need a babysitter."

"Okay—don't mean to bother you. I'll be outside doing chores if you need anything." I rake up heaps of pine needles, an always-available task renewed by every gust of wind. I keep an eye on the house, and she soon appears on the back step.

She makes her way across the yard to the picnic table. The barn cat, a dark tortoiseshell with one white whisker, sees her there and saunters up from the corral, jumps on the table. This hunter has razor claws and strong jaws, but she gently bats at a blade of grass Mom twirls in front of her.

Mom leans over to pull up more grass. "I don't even know if I'm allowed to do this. If the people here will think it's alright."

I tell her (again) that she can do whatever she likes here. It's her and Dad's place.

"It is? Well, I wish he would've asked *me* before he signed the papers."

What "me" does she mean? One she's never given voice to. It's taken dementia to loosen that one.

She talks about how Dad comes from the country, so this is natural for him to be here. But she grew up in the city. She didn't grow up like this. "Where are the sidewalks? Where are the neighbor ladies?"

It's her loneliness talking, but what to do? She doesn't remember her old friends, and with no ability to remember a fresh face and name, she can't make new ones.

$$44$$

Today she won't talk with me. While I make lunch, she sits in the living room whispering to herself, as if rehearsing or maybe pulling up out of the slough of forgetting something she can rely on.

I think about the task of walking the main irrigation ditch that runs through the ranch and takes water to properties down the slope and into the valley bottom. It was dug more than a century ago out of irregular rocky soil. Today it's four feet deep and wide in some places, mostly shallower and narrower in others, with sand accumulated on the bottom and banks held by roots of trees, rose bushes, and grass.

It takes a couple of days for the water to reach the ranch from the main headgate up the mountain. The first flow each spring brings with it last year's debris—dead leaves, sticks, and pine needles—that knits together and blocks the flow. It can stop up the entire width and depth of the ditch.

I lift out soggy clumps with a pitchfork, chasing smaller clots that drift away to collect again into bigger masses downstream. A series of ever-renewing obstructions.

Her whispering somehow reminds me of that, casting out for whatever can be retrieved. Is forgetting like the water, unstoppable, and memories the detritus moored or loosed by the banks and underwater geography? Is a mossy stone or protruding root enough to snag some needles, and then a stick, and then some leaves, and in the accumulation resist the water sweeping it all away?

45

We're all bored with each other. I don't pretend to care about the sports Dad watches. There's no conversation to be had with Mom. I'm happy to cook for them and be outside, fussing in the irrigation ditches, visiting the cat, tending the flower beds. The petunias and viola bedding plants are standing up. Seeds for wildflowers, bachelor buttons, and marigolds are pushing up through the dirt after two weeks of rainy, blowy weather. There's one more slash pile to burn, but the weather never seems right.

Up the hill, a western tanager flashes by, all yellow, orange, and black, eye-opening against green leaves. A Steller's jay swoops and scolds *kack-kack-kack-kack*. Overhead, four turkey buzzards sail on two-toned gray wings, drifting up the mountain. Yellow blossoms have burst on the caragana trees, some already dropping a confetti of petals while bumblebees and honeybees have their way. The bloom is brief. The season waits for no one.

46

Waving her hand over the lunch table, Mom questions who's "in charge of all this." She wants to know how it's been organized, how I'd become connected with them, whether I had other people I cook for. She asks with a dose of contempt, "Is this our tax dollars at work?" She thinks the lunches I make are some sort of welfare program her pride won't allow. She eats little. *She won't take charity.*

I've made the first rhubarb pie of the season, but Mom's suspicion takes the joy out of an otherwise bright moment. I smile through her questions, reassuring her that we decide together what to have for lunch, I shop for ingredients, Dad pays for them, and then I cook.

She's unconvinced and repeats, "Is this our tax dollars at work?" Dad says the pie is delicious.

47

The thing my parents value most now is a good sleep, and they mostly get it. I sleep fitfully, working out what deteriorates. Part of my task here seems to be feeling the strangeness of dementia for all of us, nodding to it, and letting it pass through without settling down.

Still, some days it's hard not to feel like I'm going out of my mind. And that has to make me laugh. It has to. The absurdity. The fuckery of memory and how the mind does and doesn't work. How even when it doesn't work, we can fool ourselves into believing it does.

At night, I watch stand-up comedy specials over and over. The funny registers in my mind, but I have to unclench before flesh will react. I know genuine laughter can keep fear at bay. Fear of what's happening to her (and eventually maybe to me).

I dream that I'm doing a stand-up routine in a small club about all this, and I'm killing. The audience is laughing with me about this grotesquely sad thing that's happening not just to Mom but also to Dad, who's unflinchingly devoted to her and just shakes his head at behavior that's increasingly bizarre and can border on dangerous. It's happening to my siblings, who deal with it in rhythms of approach and avoidance. It's happening to Mom's friends, who mark the absence of phone calls and letters. It's happening to me.

My wise friend tells me: "Two words: breathe." An absurd joke that makes me laugh (and I can't laugh without breathing).

48

My doctor tells me that signs of dementia are typically in evidence for a decade before someone gets a diagnosis. My own memory is worse for dates and names than my 90-year-old dad's. I wonder which genetic tendency I inherited and how many years it will take to show itself.

I try to mimic Dad's usual stoicism, but some days it all lands like a lead blanket, after the grocery shopping is done and the freshly split wood is stacked. It's hard to sit idle with it, but busy-ness for its own sake is a losing proposition. I can't outrun what's happening.

Mundane tasks are ticked off the list while deeper thoughts bubble in the background. I keep calm on the outside and churn on the inside. Some say I think too much, but I think as much as necessary to figure out what the hell is happening and what I can do (if anything) to respond. I balk at *either-or* and remind myself to instead ask, *yes and...?*

I dig up resources and talk to people who know more than I do, looking for enough solid ground for reasonable steps forward. I aim to help and, at the very least, do no harm.

Today, I think about my current life bookended by the life I had before and the life I'll have after this. Right now, last week, next week, next year, decades ago… all can be suddenly and equally present. In the underground parts of mind, there's little difference between past and present. It feels like a circumstantial dementia. Acceleration. Dislocation. Delamination. Floods of new information and old feeling. The unceremonious dismantling of normalcy. The wrench to identities as this comes into focus:

This person you care for is no longer the person you knew.
You need to adapt to the person she's becoming.
You need to become someone you didn't know you would be.

What's possible now? Control is an illusion. Simply being here—witness, participant, helper—is what I can do. I focus on keeping things from heading off a cliff.

49

We mark every new gap in her memory. Mourning by inches, Dad calls it.

If I focus on the gaps, I can fall right into a pit of depression. I feel the familiar pull. I look for anything that can lift us in this daily experience of what's changing. Flowers among wreckage.

50

Mom's nuanced sense of language has become more concrete. I tell her, "I'm going down to the machine shop to see what Dad's up to." She smiles and says it's funny that I'd go *down* to see what's *up*. She reads a college sports headline about the Anteaters and wonders how such small animals could possibly survive against the local Grizzlies. She calls ducks *quackers*—"you know, things that go *quack, quack*"—a creative stopgap when the word *duck* goes missing from her vocabulary.

Her crossword puzzling has become boldly transgressive. She writes several letters in one box to make a word fit in the grid. She's a woman who never got within a mile of coloring outside the lines, and I enjoy seeing this bit of freedom squirming out on the newspaper page. Wanting sometimes finds a way.

She's increasingly drawn to vivid color, whether a bright bouquet on the table or carrots on her plate. She now chooses clothes with rich reds, blazing oranges and yellows, or brilliant greens. If her subconscious could speak, I imagine it saying *fuck those decades of polite pastels.* She'd never, ever actually say that, so I'll say it: FUCK THE PASTELS.

51

One night, after I've gone home and Dad's gone to bed upstairs, she puts a plastic deli container holding a roasted chicken into the oven and turns the knob to the CLEAN setting. Lots of black smoke but Dad wakes up and gets to it before it catches fire.

I discover this the following day when I open the oven door and find the mangle of carcass and melted plastic. The tray on the bottom rack, always there to catch the bubbling fallout when baking juicy pies, kept the plastic from landing on the heating element.

A haze of panic floods me. *Smoke inhalation. Trapped upstairs by fire. They could've died.* This scenario qualifies as the kind of painful, stupid death that I moved back here to prevent.

She doesn't remember the what or why of doing it. Dad can't even speak of it, not wanting to admit that something more than usual has happened (a "more" that may require us to change how we go about caring for her). He depends on routine, and every change we make to work around her worsening condition takes him further from the way he imagined they would age, leaning on each other in the setting they recognize as home.

While I scrape up the ruin, Mom studies page one of her romance novel, ignoring me. I silently rattle through what we can do to keep everyone living here safely. I try to be clearheaded, but I'm in a tunnel, my own doing and thinking disjointed. When it's time for me to leave, I can't remember getting from house to car. *Did I put the plastic-chicken in the garbage can in the garage, like I said I would?* Some primitive brain is all lit up, body on autopilot around the limited-sight curves on the road home.

I find a home safety checklist on the Alzheimer's Association website. I go through it, make a few suggestions to Dad. He settles for status quo except for one change. He removes the control knob from the oven and hides it in the pocket of his chore coat.

52

After lunch Mom stands like stone in the front yard. She said she was going to get the mail, but plan, habit, and muscle memory all ran out halfway there.

The postal delivery driver pulls in, steps out of her car, and says hello to Mom, who doesn't recognize her anymore. I've been hovering at the side but now introduce myself to the driver, who understands dementia and keeps the conversation light.

She's delivered mail on this route for years and knows my parents well. Still, I'm surprised and touched that a driver would take the time to check on someone standing, somehow out of place, in her own front yard.

53

She wants to find her mother. Her mother's friends will know where she is. Let's call them. Then she dreams that her mother has died a grisly death. She has to tell her mother's friends. Let's call them.

She goes through this scenario again and again, torn anew every time. Her tears and distress are real, and it's no comfort to tell her that Amy died peacefully a long time ago.

It begins to seem cruel, so some days I say her mother is fine and happy. It feels strange to lie, even out of kindness to her. Or is it kindness to myself, not wanting to watch her suffer? For her, the present with no stable past or future increasingly looks like a horror film.

54

Dad has left an envelope on my placemat that he wants me to see. It's covered with Mom's scrawled handwriting declaring her fear that he means to "do her danger." She wants to see her doctor.

I ask her about it. She's bewildered. She doesn't remember writing it. Is she frightened now? No. Can she tell me what felt dangerous? No.

I tell her I'm glad she was able to write down those feelings. Letting someone else know how she's feeling is good, because that someone may be able to help. She seems to think about that. She does want to talk to her doctor, not about the danger she wrote of in the night but whether she's going out of her mind. She just can't understand why she felt like that about her beloved.

I tell her things are happening in her brain that she's not choosing. Whatever's happening doesn't always make sense, and it's not predictable. We'll do whatever we can to help her feel safe. She nods. I call the clinic for an appointment.

These distressing episodes are typical for a person with dementia, but knowing that doesn't lessen her distress. She's not in control of her thoughts. She's at the mercy of ghosts in her neurochemistry. I hope that, on balance, they'll be kind.

55

I take her to the doctor. Mom's reassured, and I bring home a prescription to discuss with Dad. Medication to manage hallucinations could help, but would she take it?

The paper prescription gets tucked away, never to be looked at again. Just like the thick information packet on dementia that the doctor gave Mom and Dad when she was diagnosed a couple of years ago. I imagine Mom and Dad coming home from the clinic that day, sitting at the table over cups of coffee, holding each other's hand, and making a silent decision to see all this through with their signature sober determination. In their mid-80s, it seemed doable.

There were no further diagnostic tests or brain scans to confirm a definitive diagnosis of Alzheimer's. Mom's diagnosis will only ever be general dementia.

There are other challenges we don't talk about. Dad is nearly blind in one eye, impairing his depth perception and making driving difficult. He's largely deaf, his hearing ruined by working around jet engines in the early years before anyone realized their noise was a hazard. He sometimes wears a hearing aid, but if he doesn't feel like listening, he leaves it out. And he has a tremor that affects his balance and fine motor control. He doesn't want to talk about it. I do enough research to feel reasonably confident that it's not Parkinson's, so I don't push it. He manages with a walking stick and turns over the check writing and correspondence to me.

56

My parents greet each other the same way every morning. One says, "It's a beautiful day." The other replies, "They're all beautiful."

I hear the deep-seated gratitude and relief of two people who were kids in the Great Depression and survived the serial uncertainty of Dad's Cold War military service, from Korea to Cuban Missile Crisis to Vietnam.

I also hear in this exchange a willed refusal of anything that might threaten their sense of a well-ordered life. It pushes complaint and doubt to the margins. It's a reminder to appreciate what is, which is also an implicit nudge not to ask for too much more.

57

It's summer, but I think about walking the labyrinth after the first snow. I prefer it then. The gray fieldstones and brown woodchip path become a landscape of small white hillocks with no message to read.

Each quadrant in the labyrinth has seven U-turns, each one at once a turning back and a moving forward. Linearity melts. In winter, a blast of cold out of the canyon fills my hood, snapping me out of any wandering nostalgia. Everything else falls away. This is what matters now.

Not unlike the feeling I had at Great Aunt Florence's bedside, an aura that wrapped the end of her life, every moment magnified, demanding as much presence as I could muster. I think about doing that vigil twice more for the people whose bodies made mine, the call to care that brought me here. Unlikely. Unexpected. Undeniable.

On that snow-blanked path, I walk with eyes fixed downward. Sun throws diamonds across the snow. It's everything until a faint squalor makes me stop. Canada geese are moving from one pond to another. I can't see them, but I hear their arc from east to south. It reminds me to look up and not lose the horizon in the urgent stream of small steps that can seize all my attention.

At the end of this, I'll be a different person. I'm learning about myself (and others) in ways I wouldn't choose. Attitudes exposed by extreme circumstance. Feelings that linger in the outer reaches. Things that fundamentally change the context I swim in and how I swim. How can I *not* be changed by what's happening here? If I emerge the same as I was, then I wasn't really here.

58

She hides her glasses then can't remember where they are. Dad pulls out the spare pair he keeps aside. She may hide those soon, too. We keep our eyes open for the first pair.

I wonder how this daily "what now?" will end. When will the work-arounds cease to work? What change will mark something that we'll no longer be able to manage at home? We're edging up to something, but there's no way to know exactly what or when.

Dementia's progression is not paint-by-number. Ongoing iterations of care are best guesses at what might answer her needs today, well-meant trial and error. Very different from the punctuation of a single choice that will mark the end of this life my parents have crafted and the beginning of something else.

I don't know how to start this conversation with Dad. He'll never consider moving her to a place for memory care, nor will he allow outside help to come in. That's one reason I'm here, to be some option to that impasse. He hopes she can die peacefully in her sleep in their shared bed. It's a beautiful wish. But can we get her there? The last stage of dementia is so much about practical bodily care.

Incontinence is a typical inflection point. Will she lose her ability to sense what her body needs, or forget that the toilet is across the hall from their bedroom, or forget what the toilet is for? All reasonable scenarios. How do I plan for it? Eat. Drink. Poop. Pee. Sleep. Can we help her with all that at home? Would she let us?

59

As usual, it's nap time after lunch. Mom rests quietly on the living room couch. Dad is upstairs in their bed.

I check on Mom, wondering if she's asleep or playing possum until I leave. Half her face looks slack.

I wake Dad from his nap. He looks at her and doesn't see it. (He doesn't want to see it.) We rouse her and sit her up. It's more obvious now. She's quiet, gazing at us, something between her usual self and a rag doll.

I ask him if I can call the ambulance. He's in charge here. It's his wife. His house. His call.

He considers. It's Saturday. The regular clinic is closed. Her doctor's not available. He suggests we let her sleep it off. Can't we wait until Monday and see how she is then?

The depth of his fear is talking. The depth of disappointment that the way they imagined dying—together, in their sleep, in their own bed —is about to be shattered. He knows, somewhere in him, that once she leaves this house she very likely won't be back. That's what he's faced with now. That phone call will change everything.

She's not in distress. We can see that on her face. Something's wrong, but she's not crying out for relief. Her brow is smooth. Maybe we can let their future here together unfold for a few more hours?

He sees that her body is limp. She won't be able to stand up, let alone walk. "If we wait," I ask, "how will we get her upstairs to bed tonight? She could sleep here, but how will we get her to the toilet? And how will we get her to the car on Monday?"

He sees the crack in the plan. This situation requires help he doesn't want and will resent when too many volunteer responders show up, the extras gawking at the crabapple trees, heavy with fruit in September, while trading the latest town gossip. He'll rail about that disrespect again and again, intruders on the moment that his world collapsed.

Ambulance. ER. ICU. She's not expected to survive the night.

Linger

60

This is not how it was supposed to go. Not in the slightest.

Dad sits in the waiting room. I'm with Mom in an ER bay, distracting her from an unruly patient on the other side of a curtain. The doctor calmly, quietly lays out the usual treatment: procedures to discover more about her current condition then reparative surgery and a period of rehab. He presents it pro forma but doesn't push it. The question in the air: Do we push on with conventional treatment, or is this the moment to choose a different path?

Eight years earlier, I had a similar conversation with a doctor about Florence. She was 100 years old and, after a heart attack, didn't want more surgery or even one more day in a hospital. Her small body was dwarfed by a voluminous hospital gown, yards of wires, and beeping sensors. Her veins were so brittle they couldn't withstand an IV. She wanted to go home.

I had her health power of attorney and refused further treatment, a surprisingly emotional decision. The signs were all clear, but the doctor kept pushing. *Shouldn't we at least discover the extent of the damage? It's a routine procedure... Most people survive it... She could add months to her life...*

The force of that white coat lecturing me to choose more intervention—over Florence's express wishes—was strong. Mercifully, a social worker suggested an alternative: hospice. Florence could go home with appropriate medical support and no more pressure for unwanted treatment.

Without question, hospice was the right path. Nevertheless, a sneaking doubt followed me around for days. The authority of fast medicine is seductive. The implicit message in that doctor's argument: *You're giving up on her. You're* choosing *death.*

From inside the medical system, ending treatment is the same as ending hope. But hope for *what* exactly? And at what cost? The risk of Florence dying on an operating table (her greatest fear) wasn't part of that doctor's calculation. At some point invasive interventions become cruelty. More is not always better.

Now, I ask the ER doctor how dementia fits into the treatment picture. What does it mean to put someone through medical procedures that they can't comprehend? To subject them to a stream of disorienting sights, sounds, smells, faces, and feelings, including pain? And—crucially—what does it mean to put someone through all that when they can't hold an understanding that the discomfort and alien goings-on are in service of feeling better tomorrow?

In the ever-present *now* of Mom's mind, anxiety is anxiety. Fear is fear. Pain is pain, with no idea why or for how long. What's the difference between that and torture?

It's time for slow, hands-on, empathetic care rather than fast, high-tech intervention based on statistical probabilities and a medical chart. Hospice seems the best path forward. Dad agrees.

61

I stay with Mom overnight in the ICU. She rests comfortably, left side slack. She's not on any medication and shows no signs of pain. She hasn't spoken but is vaguely alert.

I call my three siblings in turn and put the phone up to her ear, so she can hear their voices. It's a chance for last words before each trundles into a plane or car to get here as quickly as they can, hoping she'll still be here by the time they arrive. I've been warned that the first stroke may soon be followed by more.

The nurse knows we're waiting for hospice admission to be approved. She's glad that Mom will be able to go to the hospice center with dedicated staff rather than go home, where Dad and I would become her always-on caregivers.

"This gives you a chance to be her daughter, and your father to be her husband, rather than the pressures of being her nurse," she says. I didn't know then how right she was.

62

Before parts of her and my father collided, I was nothing. No *thing*. No *where*. She made me into something. *What* exactly is still up in the air.

Now, with night quiet settling in, I think about how some-thing slides back toward no-thing. The moment between last breath and no breath. I watch her chest rise and fall. Something hovers.

63

Florence declined through what hospice workers called a remarkably lucid process of active dying. I took her home to her assisted living apartment, trailed by a portable oxygen tank. She was relieved. A return to normalcy, though it wasn't normal at all.

She was allowed to stay in her apartment, rather than be moved to the complex's hospital-like wing, as long as I stayed with her 24/7. Her heartbeat was strong and steady (as it was to her last breath), other vital signs also good.

She combed her hair, aware that she wasn't as put together as she liked to be. She wanted to sit in an armchair looking toward her open door, so she could see people passing by and they could see her. She wanted their hello's, especially from her best friend Marcie across the hall.

She needed constant reorientation: *What day is it? What time of day is it? What's happened to me? Why do I feel like this? Why do I need oxygen?* She'd been healthy so much of her life that she just didn't know what to make of the strange new state of things.

In the apartment, the portable canister was replaced by a chugging oxygen concentrator (dubbed "the Harley" by the head nurse). Florence felt responsible for making sure that it worked properly. She frequently checked the tubing from canula to machine, fretting, "Am I hooked up?" She worried that she didn't know its maintenance routine. *Did she need to clean a filter? How often? Where would she buy one?* Self-sufficiency is part of the family code. I come by it honestly.

64

Dad and I sit at the kitchen table filling out hospice admission paper-work with Michelle, the hospice social worker. She's quietly intense, attentive and inviting. Her manner says that there's all the time in the world, while she somehow also gets things done without delay.

She asks him if Mom has a will. No. Does he have a will? He delivers his usual line: "No. The kids can fight over it." Michelle glances at me. I shrug.

I doubt Dad really want his kids to fight (I certainly don't want to). Fights over inheritance are always, at some level, about love. Who got the most stuff (and most love)? Who feels cheated of stuff (and love)? Questions about relationship status and place in the family that can't be voiced or even felt directly—too vulnerable, too raw, too complicated, a bleeding heart that might be mistaken for a weak heart—surface. Material goods and love, two incommensurables, get weighed on the same scale. Inheritance becomes proof of love or its lack.

I wonder if it works the other way around, too. Does Dad enjoy the idea of us kids fighting over his stuff because it proves we value *him?* I wonder if Dad needs to hear that we love him for more than what he'll leave behind?

I also wonder if his distaste for lawyers stands in the way of making a will. He tells me he was once cheated out of $5,000 by a lawyer who turned out to be a grifter (after that, Mom managed the money). So I download some forms, draft a basic will, have a lawyer friend look it over for disastrous mistakes, and Dad signs it. It's more a statement of intent than an enforceable edict. It's a start of a more specific conversation that his executor could but never will have. It's a North Star, and later our aim will be for shit.

Dad and I also put a power of attorney and advance directives in place. He's seen our lucky escape from unwanted medical intervention for Mom. He assumed that he could speak for her, but state law has changed recently. The small local hospital took his direction, but in a larger hospital system, we would've been in for a fight.

He hopes for the best, while I guard against the worst. He's not sure he trusts anyone but himself. Still, he's seen me make decisions for Mom that he agreed with. I might be his best bet to navigate a decline neither of us wants to imagine.

65

By the next afternoon, hospice has been approved, and a bed from the hospice wing is wheeled down the hall to the ICU. Mom is transferred to it, and we start the short trip back.

The bed rolls smoothly guided by Ed, a seasoned hospice nurse who usually tends patients in the field. He bends a little, his tall frame moving us steadily down the hall. Most of the hospice rooms are empty, but we pass one where a man moans loudly. Ed glances at me, round glasses intensifying his gaze, and explains—matter-of-fact but not without care—"He's having a hard time."

Her quiet room feels more mid-tier hotel than hospital, with couch, recliner, homey décor, and large windows looking onto green space. As he parks her bed next to the nightstand, Mom says she sees a beautiful angel swimming across the ceiling. Another angel sits in the corner over the door, watching her.

I look up, tracking her gaze, and see an evocative shape by a sprinkler head. "Do you mean that shadow?"

Before she can reply, Nurse Ed says, "Or maybe she sees an angel."

Memories of Florence wash in, and what Ed means lands: Here, Mom's perceptions lead. Given the profoundly unknowable change she's undergoing, why not angels? Why not the appearance of things only she can see? Why not visions that are meaningful and comforting? (And what a relief that they are. Some people in this liminal space see frightening things.)

Why not accept what she sees in this transition that we'll all experience and will always escape understanding? I take a deep breath and feel a wave of the hands-on-but-hands-off care that Florence taught me. Close attention to practical needs and openness to the unexpected. I remember that dying has its own obscure logic. My job is less about knowing and more about affirming. *Yes—and?*

66

Mom tells the nurse that Ed is also her father's name. "Well," he says, "you know what they say. Two Eds are better than one." Her face screws up, half groan, half laugh. Her sense of humor is intact.

She hasn't eaten for a day and a half, and swallowing may be an issue. She can have pureed foods and thickened liquids, taken slowly. She isn't able to feed herself. At this time of day, applesauce and chocolate pudding are on offer. Without a doubt: chocolate pudding.

I'm schooled in helping her with slow, small bites. Speed is the enemy of safety. A leisurely pace minimizes the chance of silent aspiration, food or drink going down the wrong pipe. Ed tells me that aspiration causes choking and invites pneumonia and even death. Who knew pudding could kill you?

67

I bring Dad to visit. The siblings arrive with son, daughters, and new son-in-law in tow. Dad frowns at the "circus." He's glad to see them, but this rare gathering is too clear a sign that something significant is happening. No one can pretend that any of this is routine, and Dad relies on routine for his own peace of mind. We're in another dimension now.

68

My wise friend has warned me about what he calls "the crazy sibling chapter." Not a prediction about mine in particular but what happens to families in general, how extreme circumstances can churn up every old wound, unresolved longing, expectation, grudge, and complaint. Elsewhere in the world we may have matured, but in the room facing our mother's death, we're children again, with all the underground dynamics, alliances, and antagonisms intact. Even the closest families can become strained, and we're not a close family.

Who sits near the bed? Who learns how to safely feed her? Who talks around or over her? Who's bewildered by that woman lapping up all the attention while not attending to us? Who finds it easier to plan her funeral than see their mother in the half-slack face? Who reassures themselves that she'll go to heaven *because Jesus?* Who leaves once it's clear that we're all strangers to her, none more special than the others?

No one wants to measure the chasm between an ideal of her that's lodged in their heads and who lays on the bed, a woman whose gaze now asserts a different demand on us.

Can I see *her?* Or can I only see myself reflected by her?

It's hard to see the woman who's still *becoming* within the woman who's *dissolving.* It's easy to miss the woman who's emerging. It's easy to insist on who she *was,* because that's the woman we still want (or need) her to be. We'll repeat a version of this fragmented drama when Dad declines.

69

I'd like to tell a story about all this. I'd like to connect these dots in a way that shimmers with promise, meaning, and sense. It would be such a comfort.

I can't comfort anyone. Every story is a fragment. Every line that pretends at cause and effect is a partial lie. Things happen. Some things happen near each other for no particular reason. Dumb luck plays a part.

Piecing things together with string and revelation is a fool's game. The mind's aperture is baffled by the heart. *How much can I stand to hear? How much can I tolerate knowing?*

Rashomon comes to mind, Akira Kurosawa's iconic film of an event recounted by four different people, resulting in four very different stories. We all come to her bedside—four kids with, in some ways, four different mothers. Circumstances and she herself changed as each of us came into the family. My oldest brother was born a year after Mom and Dad were married. Their first home was a small travel trailer at Mountain Home Air Force Base in Idaho, not the life my college-educated mother might've imagined when she fell in love with the young captain. But pictures show her beaming. They were a handsome couple.

By the time I came along, seven years later, two more kids had arrived and the family had moved to Rapid City, South Dakota, where Dad worked out of Ellsworth Air Force Base. Then three years in Hawaii, living in Kailua on Oahu while Dad worked out of the military base at Kaneohe Bay. The Vietnam War was escalating, but I was three and oblivious, reveling in a world of friendly strangeness. Praying mantis camouflaged against my hair. My face pressed eye level with the sleeping grass that closed when I waved my hand over it. Big Bufo toads under the banana trees. Manta rays following me along the aquarium glass at Sea Life Park. Other kids to play with who didn't look or sound like me.

After my siblings were all in school, Mom and I had a couple years of days to ourselves. We had sundaes at Liberty House department store in Honolulu. *We can have sundaes when it's Monday?* She tried not to laugh when I'd pick up the phone and call my "friend" (the female voice of the time and temperature recording) to tell her why I was mad at Mom. To make up, we colored together. I was lucky. I had her to myself for a couple of years and was old enough to appreciate it.

Then the family moved to Colorado for the year-plus that Dad was in Vietnam and Thailand (to me, just places on a map). Only years later did I find the base layer of shock in the unspeakable realization that Dad may never have come home. Maybe I was the only one in the family who never got hold of that idea at the time. We moved through the days and nights as if he would come home. Always *as if.*

I learned *as if* too well. I learned how to wait, part of me absorbing a way of being from Mom's waiting body, sitting in the living room then as she did in these later years, staring out the window, winnowing thoughts and sifting fears. *Waiting* as both means and end.

She had a recurring dream for the year that they were engaged, when he was stationed in Korea. She had to find him in a vast warehouse of tall crates. Every time she caught a glimpse of him, he'd round a corner and be gone again. She taught me to treasure glimpses of what I might want while doing the work of waiting.

A great deal of imagination is required to withstand the quiet stress of waiting. Mom had an immense capacity for it, though I saw the absence when she disappeared into herself. Maybe that was a more hospitable place to sit things out until Dad returned and something like family life resumed.

The siblings saw other things in her. We're each very different people. She tried to give us each what we needed. No one knows everything, and no one's relationship with her is definitive.

Now, as capacities dwindle and surge, several of her selves quietly compete for attention. I feel the ways I can never know her, as none of us really knows the other, even when that other is your mother.

And that's as it should be. I can't neatly sum her up. I respect her. I guard her dignity. She always foregrounded domestic sweetness, but I know her imagination is unspeakably wild.

70

First things first. We bring her nightgowns from home and split the back from hem to torso, to make it easier for nurses to change her brief. "Brief"—a term meant to be kind but wholly inadequate to combat her indignant awareness that she's now wearing a diaper.

I stay overnight with her, helping with supper and routines at bedtime and waking up, while my sister stays during the day. We expect that we'll be here a matter of days or a few weeks.

71

She's dabbling in some unknown, but she's also dabbling with us and our uncertainties about ourselves, our relationships with her, the meat of her life, her not-quite-thinkable death—all that stuff that's difficult to talk about without sounding trite or impossibly mysterious. The most honest thing I can say now is a shrug.

Simply put, she's going somewhere we can't follow. All our confidence in caring for her—*I know what she needs*—is useless. There's no mission we can complete. She, in her failing body, is now the strongest one in the room. Of this, I'm certain (the only thing of which I'm certain).

The unknowable stalks the room. I can't name it. All I can do is listen for demands to be heard through the body on the bed.

72

The blank wall by her door is, for her, something like a movie screen. She sees writing on it in a foreign language she doesn't understand. She sees figures "in old-time dress" strolling across it, one of them walking a dog, in a place that's like a park. She reports all this with light curiosity.

Surreal images slowly materialize, demanding only awe. Is she wandering in that liminal space between here and not-here? I remember such visions from Florence's last weeks, when she saw her parents and other figures she asked for instruction: "What's my next priority?"

Mom says her dreams are "weird." She can't "sift" them. "I'm not sure if they're dreams or if I was in an otherworldly… place." She sees her mom and dad. They can help her get to where she needs to go, she says, "when the time is right."

73

Within days, it's clear that Mom's memory is much the same, though the distressing hallucinations she had during the summer seem to be gone. She often knows who Dad is and wants his company.

But her personality has shifted. A dry wit has emerged. Her tongue is freed, less cautious in word and manner. "Sassy," she says with a grin. She sounds more like her mother.

74

Friends from her teaching days visit. She remembers teaching more than having had children or decades of family life. She jokes with them: *You know those people who're a burr under your saddle? What about writing a letter to them, saying what you really think, and then having it mailed to them right after you die? What do you think of that?*

Telling someone off (even politely) is a delicious idea. But what, I wonder, can she say *only* if she's guaranteed the last word? What thought is so devastating that she doesn't even want to be alive for the reply, whether defense or apology?

Later, I ask her, "Am I still one of the burrs under your saddle?" She ignores the question. I tell her that I hope she'd tell me, so I have a chance to repair things between us.

For a moment, she looks confused. A ripple of a new thought? Could something *good* happen after she lets her true feelings be heard? (Am I still a stranger or, for a moment, her daughter?)

Then the familiar face, an actor's composed calm. "That'll never happen," she says. Indeed.

75

Small things emanate secret meanings to her. She plays hide-and-seek with joy.

She explores the texture of the jersey bedsheet, newly pleasurable. She runs a finger over the hand-embroidered stitching on the crazy quilt that covers her bed. Her mother made the squares. She runs a hand over the fabrics, lingering over some more than others.

When Mom was a kid, her mother fostered babies for weeks at a time, nursing the sick ones back to health on their way to adoption or providing respite for distressed parents. Mom saw babies come and go from the house, each with a small bundle of clothes. She told me once that she saw her mother's devotion to them—*what a fierce love!*—and yet felt a sinister doubt that one day a car would arrive for her, revealing that she, too, was a foster child. *Who would take care of her then?*

She smiles because she sees babies crawling across the ceiling. She says they seem happy, but she wonders who takes care of them.

76

When a nurse comes in to change her brief, Mom plays dead, weak limbs with strong bones heavy on the bed. She keeps her eyes closed, but her mouth purses tighter and tighter until no lips are visible. She looks now most like a stereotypical old person, dentures gone, lips a barely visible puckered line.

But Mom has all her teeth. In fact she's quite proud of how well she cares for her teeth. Her pucker is a sign of disapproval, the one we must read from her face, because she will never put words to it.

77

Mom has a doll collection from her growing up years, an era of life that she regularly inhabits. I bring one of the soft ones, thinking she may recognize and enjoy it.

Wrong. She pushes it away with the imperious look I recognize from the day I proposed the coloring book. I put the doll on her bedside table. Maybe I chose the wrong moment. Maybe I'll try again later.

The next day I find the doll on the floor. A hospice volunteer had the same idea, the result an unequivocal message.

She seems to be many of her past selves all at once, and any one of them may speak. But her dignity and sense of adult authority hold them all together. She's diminished and may find her mind in the place of childhood, but she's no child.

78

Muscle memory takes over. Brushing her teeth. Brushing her hair. Holding a newspaper. She can't start the activity or ask for it, but if it's suggested, she can pick it up. It reminds me that I should be conscious of the habits I'm building now. They may be what's left to prop me up at the end.

Sometimes she gets stuck in the routine. As she brushes her teeth, we do a comical dance over the kidney dish where I encourage her to spit out the rinse water. "Swish, swish, swish, spit," I say, holding the dish near her chin.

She's focused, staring fixedly at the wall. *Swish swish swish …* and where *spit* should be, more *swish swish swish swish swish swish swish swish swish swish swish swish swish swish … swallow.*

She smiles at me. Cheeky.

79

After some weeks, the strength on her left side returns. She swallows more evenly. She speaks more clearly. She hasn't had another stroke. Is she recovering?

This is good news. Still, everything is a mixed sack of emotional rocks. One evening after supper, she asks stock questions about Dad: Is he watching a baseball game? Is he getting enough to eat? Then, after a long silence, turns her head to stare at the tall cupboard door next to her bed: "Is that coffin empty?"

Some evenings, when I say goodbye to her, she has tears in her eyes. For a minute or an hour, she seems to know far more than she wants to, and it hurts.

80

I walk the labyrinth to remember myself. Today I'm struck by all the U-turns. Fifty-six total to the center and back out. For the last few weeks, I've been asking myself what it will take for her to accomplish a good death. Now I take a mental U-turn: What, in her new condition, is a good life?

She can stay in hospice up to three months, and then she'll need to go somewhere else. Back home? A new care setting? How fully will she recover? Will she walk again? What physical ability can she regain as her brain continues to deteriorate?

Figuring this out will require a thought exercise about house retrofits and the cost of in-home caregivers. And if that isn't feasible, the next path: an educated guess about the level of care that will suit her, with appropriate introductions and tours of care facilities, interviews with admissions staff, medical assessments, cost assessments, etc.

We calculate what Dad's finances can sustain. Her doctor says that she's seen patients in Mom's condition live for five days or five years.

81

Before supper, I give her a pedicure and trim her hair. After supper, she throws off the covers and announces, "Well, I think I'm done here." She enjoyed this day at the spa, but it's time to go home. Dad must be wondering where she is. She points to the wall and asks, "Is that the exit?"

I tuck her back in and explain that she's at the hospice center, and this is where she sleeps. "Is that from tonight? I don't know anything about that."

A few minutes later she again throws off the covers and says she'll just walk home, since I'm not helping her get there. When she says "home," she means the ranch, not the house where she was a teenager. That's different.

82

We pass the two-month mark. I tell myself it's doable. *Doable* is my aim. I gas up the car before the gauge drops to E. I get makeup on both eyes. My socks match.

I pick up Dad at 9 a.m. and drive us fifteen miles to the hospice center. Settle him in a chair at Mom's bedside with a half cup of coffee. Wait in the hallway for about an hour while they have private time together. Go back in the room, make some small talk, ask Dad if it's time to go (a decision he leaves me to make for us all). Drive Dad home. Let the dog out. Refill the woodbox. Shake ripe apples off one of the trees for the deer. Ask Dad if he'd like some lunch (always yes but still important to ask). Negotiate the menu. Pull lunch together. Eat. Talk about what needs doing. Add Dad's requests to the grocery list. Get the mail from the mailbox. Wash dishes. Do a little housekeeping (scrub a toilet, wash out a sink, refill soap containers, sweep the floor, do a load of laundry ... one or two tasks a day keeps the house livable). Say goodbye to Dad, who's on his way upstairs for a nap. Visit the barn cat. Drive back up the hill to my place for a couple of hours. Check my mailbox, personal and business e-mail, voicemail, and text messages (mercifully, most clients have gone silent). Walk the labyrinth or call a friend. Around 4 p.m., drive back alone to the hospice center. Check in with the nurse on duty. Any changes or concerns? Spend time with Mom looking at greeting cards or reading aloud from letters or a book. Help the nurse when Mom's brief needs changing. Help her with supper, brought on a tray. Putter around after supper for a half hour while she stays sitting up to aid digestion. Help with her bedtime routine, brushing teeth and hair, smoothing on face cream and lotion on legs and arms. Read aloud a little more. Have a little chat. Put on some calm music. Close the shades, turn off the lights. Kiss her goodnight. Drive home. Breathe.

83

I take time to sit quietly with Mom once she's ready for sleep. We've rolled relentlessly through the day, with frequent interruptions for the practical tasks of bodily care. Nurses are quiet and unobtrusive, but they're still strangers (visitors?) Mom works to put into the frame of this place that she knows isn't home. All of that can crowd out a budding thought.

I ask if there's anything she's wondering about or anything I can help with. Anything on her mind? Most days she's guarded. But the faint *whoosh* from the public toilet on the other side of the wall might turn her head. *What is that?* The bed's electric motor whirrs, cycling to keep the mattress at its correct firmness. *What is that?*

Occasionally she asks how her mom is doing.

As I leave, I kiss her and wish her a good sleep. She and I have always shared the experience of colorful dreams with thick plots. I remind her that if she wants to talk to anyone in her dreams, she can think about them as she falls asleep. It's like an invitation. She says, "You're welcome in my dreams anytime."

I stroke her hair, throat suddenly full. Everything is doable but this emotional crush. "I'll try to visit." I close the shades, turn off the lamp, and realize I need to say one more thing to her: "And you're welcome in my dreams anytime." She smiles and closes her eyes.

84

"How're you doing?" friends ask.

I reach for words, but none fit. Turns out I don't really know. I walk on ground where I grew up, but for so many reasons I mostly feel dislocated. I'm doing so many things I've never done before and may never do again. The kinds of things that don't bear too much introspection but do require some sort of recognition.

I remind myself that too much knowingness is a problem here. Admitting what I don't know—including naming what I feel—is at least honest.

Someone reminds me of the saying that you can't read a label from inside the jar. I'm definitely *inside it* now. But I'm not without resources. Years ago, a therapist advised *don't confuse uncertainty with incompetence.*

I don't know everything, but I know enough. Better now to simply look. The power of a gaze can change things that seem otherwise impenetrable. I look a lot these days.

85

And for all my sense that yes, this is doable, on some days, preoccupied with the day's list to come, my own mundane routine becomes fragile. I haven't walked the labyrinth for days. I haven't checked in with friends as often as I should. I forget to check the mail.

These things are crowded out by the situation at the ranch and at the hospice center. The squatters I've welcomed into my mental space occupy me.

Clawing back my morning routine—*remember to take your vitamins*—I realize that I don't usually *think* about taking my vitamins. I do that in a string of other things that happen from waking to getting to work. Shower, clothes, makeup, breakfast, vitamins... one act calls up the next, until the whole introduction to the day is done. But now my mind drifts, ends up wondering why Dad was angry yesterday or what it means that Mom's angels seem to have vanished.

What I take for granted in that early routine isn't conscious mastery. It's actually a sly blend of habit, repetition, and a dash of attention, so familiar that the actual effort fades to background.

Now everything is foreground. Every day disrupted. Habits are harder to inhabit. Daily life takes more work. I need more attention than I have right now. Some days a part of me slips through the cracks. That's not sustainable, but what to do?

86

Every morning, I make a list on paper for the day and tuck it into a vest pocket, a touchstone. My list is more detailed lately, because the act of writing helps to retain the memory. And the most difficult things (logistically, emotionally, or both) need to be written down so I can't get to the end of the day having let them disappear into my back of beyond.

I write a periodic email to the siblings to update them on Mom's condition. *Is it time to do that again?* Dad has asked me to source a load of logs for firewood, a specific type of timber at a specific (unreasonably low) price. *Where do I even start?* Someone mentions a new option for a care home. *Make the appointment for a tour.*

Every evening, I review the list and cross off everything done. What remains is the start of the next day's list. Crossing off items gives me a brief shot of satisfaction. An exhale. If I've done things that aren't on the list I sometimes add them, simply for the pleasure of crossing them off. On a rough sea of a day, small accomplishments are buoys.

87

A month ago, she wasn't expected to last the night. Or the next day. Or the day after that. She seemed to be leaning toward another dimension. Then the lid of a chocolate pudding snack was peeled back, and the aroma made her nose twitch. *That other place can wait.*

Chocolate has power. It was the same with Florence. It will be the same with Dad.

After eating some chocolate ice cream, she burps a burp bigger than any I've ever heard from her. She looks shocked. Such a sound from her own body! I laugh, "Good one!" She sees my enjoyment and decides she can enjoy it, too. Chocolate was always a pleasure Mom snuck when everyone else was out of the house. Now, she relishes it openly.

Once, at the family dinner table during my early teen years, Dad declared that he'd had enough to eat. Mom replied quietly, "I've never felt full in my life." I don't know if anyone else heard her or, if they did, had any idea of the bottomless despair in that simple statement. I knew, because I was living it, too.

It would take years to put form to the feelings, that gaping hunger that had nothing to do with food and the shameful fat that lamented *if only we had more willpower... or were anorexic instead of overeaters... or had the metabolism of a hummingbird... but at least we aren't alcoholics.* That's something like how the logic goes.

In the wreckage of dementia and stroke, leaving that baggage behind is an unexpected gift. Taking pleasure in food and her body—openly— will be an accomplishment of her last months.

88

As weeks pass, her wit mostly goes back into hiding. Her keen social acuity returns, a careful approach to conversation that can still fool the casual visitor into believing that her memory is perfectly intact.

If someone wants to believe that she knows them, she offers a path to that comforting illusion. I've never wanted that from her. I wake up each day wondering what part of her will show itself. What self is still hungry to be seen?

89

She doesn't like having her soaked or smeared brief changed. The indignity is hard to shake afterward. She dislikes being turned every four hours (like a roasting chicken, she says) to avoid pressure sores. Her brow furrows, and her lips purse.

I say, "I know it's not much fun being stuck in bed."

She draws herself up, a little surprised, a touch indignant. "I find enough to enjoy myself."

An easy mistake: To weigh her quality of life now against the woman she used to be. Or measure it by the distance between her prime and this quiet moment. Today she is exactly the self she can be.

90

Mom tries to pick out the original among increasing duplicates and fakes. Dad tells me that before she altogether forgot who I was, she thought there were at least three of me. Every time I called on the phone, this added another duplicate. She insisted on it.

She points at the thermostat. "Is that the authentic one?"

I hand her a paper napkin before supper. "Is this real?" she asks.

I suggest that everything she's experiencing is real to her, and that's what matters. Instead of worrying about what's real or not, is there a way to take pleasure in the things she sees and hears and thinks now? Can it all be useful or enjoyable?

I tell her this, while I wonder about the puzzle of multiple dimensions she's trying to work out. Life as hall of mirrors.

91

"Where am I?" *The hospice center.*

"How long have I been here?" *Seventy days.*

"Why am I here?" *You had a stroke, and now this is the best place for us to care for you.*

"Don't leave me here."

An hour later, she can't remember the conversation and seems content with where she is, or is at least not willing to betray her suspicion that things are not as they should be.

Another day she says, "I'm bewildered! What is this place?" She's sure I've been keeping secrets from her.

This between-place seems the worst. Not the relatively calm and endless *now* of dementia nor the place of full consciousness, where one thought leads to the next, conclusions can be reached, and resolutions can be made and kept. In this between-place, she repeatedly discovers that life has taken her somewhere she never wanted to go.

Once, I tell her about the stroke, ER, ICU, and now hospice. She says, "I don't remember any of that. I guess it's good I don't remember that." I have to agree.

92

In the post-supper quiet time, she hears men's voices in the hallway. "Are your brothers home?"

That surprises me. *She thinks she's home? She knows she has children? And she knows I'm her kid?*

Then asks, "When did your mother pass away?"

I tell her my mother is somewhere between living and dying, trying to find her way.

"Oh. Is your father still alive?"

I say, "Yes, and he's hanging on to make sure my mother's taken care of."

"Oh."

It's all a punch to the gut, and I wonder how direct I should be. *You're recovering from a stroke, but your mind is still deteriorating, taking your body with it by degrees.* Is that what she needs me to say to her? It's medically true, but today she feels herself to be full of life. Why disrupt that?

93

She worries, "I don't even know when the first day of school is." I tell her the school year started a couple of months ago, and all the students have teachers and are learning what they need to learn. She hasn't missed a class. She doesn't need to worry.

I ask if she's had any dreams. "Oh, just the usual before the start of the school year, making sure my room and lessons are ready." Her mind has taken her to the place where she was successful and valued for her own professional accomplishments. It must be a better place to be than in this dreamlike place that is hospice, with its shifting cast of characters, hushed comings and goings, and occasional boisterous burst from the family of a patient down the hall.

94

As Dad and I are leaving, I ask if she wants anything. She looks hard at me, mouth moving in her characteristic working-up-to-say-something expression, then urges me, "You offspring. You take care of Dad. He won't ask for anything."

I assure her that I'm doing my best. Making sure the woodbox is full, the walk is shoveled, the bills are paid, the fridge is full, the satellite dish and TV are working, the laundry is done... I help him get whatever he wants, which lately has meant sourcing new winter boots, a shoehorn, and a set of screwdrivers.

95

Mom is tucked in for the night. Her favorite Enya CD plays quietly. As I get ready to leave, she says, "You're such a solace." She's had an embarrassing afternoon, a mess in her brief, and she keenly felt the lack of dignity in the whole situation.

She's always been so private and independent about her self-care. So I've helped her to feed herself and brush her own hair and teeth, to restore some sense of doing for herself. But helping her understand the call button is a non-starter. She can call up old routines but not learn new ones. She depends on us to know or guess what she needs and make it all as lighthearted as we can.

She doesn't want me to leave. She asks me little questions to keep the conversation in play.

"Are you missing your supper?" *No, I'll have supper after I get home.*

"How long are you staying?" *For as long as you and Dad need me.*

"Where do you live?" *Up the hill from the ranch.*

"We should just bring you home and adopt you."

She holds my hand more firmly than usual, stroking it with her thumb. *Should I stay longer? Until she falls asleep?* A previous self would decide then and there to stay as long as necessary. But earlier this afternoon I got some exercise and remembered a bit of myself that had gone missing. I'm tired. I need sleep. If I stay longer, will that small light of self that shone today wink out?

I put her hand under the covers, but she sneaks it out and captures mine again. I untangle our hands and use mine to stroke her hair, running my fingers through and flipping it at the ends the way I've seen her do countless times. She closes her eyes. She likes this so much that she begins to stroke her fingers against her other palm. We do this for three songs, then I kiss her forehead.

Her eyes fly open. "Are you packing it in?"

"I need to go home to have my supper and go to bed. Maybe I'll see you in your dreams." She says nothing. "Is there anything you need?"

"I just need... ... ... to say how much I appreciate getting to know you."

A strange thing to hear from your mother. We somehow see each other with more honesty and vulnerability (on both sides) than we ever could in earlier years. It took forgetting enabled by dementia (hers) and psychotherapy (mine) to make it possible.

I leave wondering if this was the lesson for today—that taking breaks from each other is not a threat to ongoing love. Any act of leaving has always been freighted with a tinge of finality. The return is never guaranteed. That's what a military wife learns. That's what this military kid learned. Tonight I go home to care for myself, and tomorrow I'll be back to see her, until one of us is no longer here to be seen.

96

Sunset comes early this time of year. When clouds momentarily clear the half moon, light floods the ground. My silent body casts a shifting shadow in the labyrinth.

I used to walk hill trails in the chaparral landscape north of Los Angeles. People typically hike those trails with a brisk pace and outward enthusiasm, chatting, pointing at the vistas deep into the hills to the west and shrieking when they come across a resident rattlesnake.

I think now of a woman I used to see, always walking alone, with hands clasped behind her back, leaning forward slightly in a measured, unhurried, relentless motion. No grasping or reaching is possible with hands so occupied. I clasp mine behind my back now, feel my chest open, and walk. I don't miss watching for snakes.

The sprint of ER, ICU, and hospice has melted into a marathon. I ask what needs to be done that only I can do, and I do that. That's why I returned, and why I'm still here.

I'm aware how often I reach my limit. Then move the boundary of that limit to make more space for what needs thinking or doing.

And after all the scenario planning in the dark, the endless if/then exercise, every day begins with one foot on the floor by the bed. Slowly, so as not to twist an ankle.

Then the other foot on the floor, scenarios dissolving into a half-thought wish that I will be whatever the day demands. A commitment to meet the day on its own terms, with care, thought, patience, and compassion. I won't speak of love. That comes later.

97

Mom's graduating from hospice. Where to next?

Dad and I sort through the situation, consider every aspect we can think of, ask nurses and others to tell us what we're missing. It all revolves around the primary question: What's best for her?

The pay from Dad's military retirement and Mom's teaching, used frugally over the years, means finances aren't an immediate worry. (I think about all the people, like me, born after that era of decent pension plans who will, facing this situation, have to make do in other ways.)

Can she come home? She won't be able to go up and down the stairs, so we'd need to modify the living room to accommodate a hospital bed. We talk to the neighbor who built Dad's machine shop. He could help us with a refit. I look into renting a lift. The county senior services agency can lend small equipment like a bedside commode.

Then I think about how happy she seems in a certain swirl of company, chatting with new faces. Back home, I expect she'll return to staring out the window at trees, mountains, and sky, likely commenting, as she did over and over the previous summer, how still it all is.

She's bedbound, but could she learn to walk again? Should she be getting up in the morning, dressed, and into a wheelchair? I find out the cost of a home health aide who could help with the morning routine. The rest of the day and night would be on Dad and me. Siblings might help, but no one lives close enough to rely on. I try to imagine how this would feel a year in, deep into winter. I'm not sure I can do it. I'm not sure what it would do to Dad.

The best fit of care facility would be West Hills Assisted Living, a small family-run home near the hospice center. They don't have an opening. I add Mom to the waiting list and ask if I can stay in touch, in case the situation changes. Dad wants a room there to open up, but he says he doesn't want to wish anyone dead.

Investigating the other care situations within driving distance of the ranch makes my stomach churn, from hard-surfaced, industrial-strength institutions to small, dank places. Dad doesn't go on these tours with me. He finds the idea of Mom (and by proxy himself) living in such places too grim.

98

Mom moves to the skilled nursing wing of a licensed nursing home, a holding place until a room opens up at West Hills. Some thirty-five people are part of her wing, a number that will swell to near fifty by the time she leaves. She starts a new routine of being dressed each morning and going to the communal dining room in a wheelchair to have breakfast. Then a group activity, then toileting, then a snack, then a nap, then lunch, then a nap, then a snack, then toileting, then dinner, then undressing, then sleep.

She sighs over being asked to "jump through hoops," while worrying that she's broken into this room and is living here illegally. "What about surveillance?" she asks. She expects that at any moment someone will come in to arrest her.

The blocky, institutional architecture and tinny sounds bouncing off hardwearing floors and walls make her think she's in a public building of some sort. Not a home. Why would we leave her to sleep in such a place?

99

She's not strong enough to stand, but she shifts her feet off the edge of the bed, as if readying to get up. If she gets her legs out too far, she could fall to the floor. Her bed in the hospice center had rails that could be raised to keep her safe. In the state-licensed nursing home, rails are considered a restraint. Restraints aren't allowed (for good reason). What to do?

Her bed is in a corner, with one long open side. Each night, the bed is lowered so she's about a foot off the floor. I bring a foam fall mat to cushion the linoleum next to the bed.

We source a scooped mattress for her. The shape doesn't prevent her from getting out of bed, but it takes enough extra effort that simply dangling her legs over the side won't bring the rest of her with them. The scooped shape also makes it easier for her to sleep on her side.

Rumor is the state will soon declare scooped mattresses a form of restraint. The nursing home will be happy to sell us this one, and we'll take it to West Hills. Small assisted living facilities operate under different state regulations that allow for more customization and, as it will turn out, more mercy.

100

I visit twice a day. Dad visits every other day. He needs a day between visits to recover from the long walk down the hallway to Mom's room, past the open doors of people in their waning days. Some sit in the hallway, slumped over in their wheelchairs. "Inmates," he calls them, "in God's waiting room."

101

A big cottonwood has fallen across the irrigation ditch. Dad gets on the tractor and tells me to fetch the chainsaw.

He drags the trunk to solid ground, then points to the places he wants me to cut it. He yells through the deafening buzz that I'm not sawing it up right. I shut off the chainsaw.

He says he could do a better job if only… I hold the chainsaw out to him. He says he can't start it. I say I'll start it for him. He doesn't want to get sawdust on his clean clothes. I say I'll do laundry.

I start the saw and carefully hand it to him. He makes a cut no better or worse than mine, and it becomes clear that he doesn't really care about the cuts at all. He needs to yell at something about anything other than our helplessness in the face of Mom's situation. A solid tree trunk and I will do.

I stand by, trying not to take it personally, but when your father yells at you, it's difficult not to feel, in some part, like a child again. Today, I'll need to walk the labyrinth. But now, the tree will get cut to size then those chunks rolled into the tractor bucket and stacked by the red woodshed. Even rage can have a constructive side.

102

I watch the fire I've started in the burn barrel. The fire and I seethe. I walk the labyrinth. The trees and I sigh.

But mostly I don't want to be angry. I don't want to react to any of the situations that *push push push* my buttons. I need to stay in a constructive frame of mind.

Mom's behavior has become the easiest to let go. There's not even anything to forgive, because she's not responsible anymore. She's just trying to survive what must feel like a surreal daily grind.

Dad's a different story. But he needs empathy, too. I see how hard it is for him to leave her in this place he knows she doesn't want to be.

103

Before Mom moved into the nursing home, I had the wall-mounted TV removed from her room. Jumping action, babbling voices, shows, commercials, talking heads... it's become a mindboggling test. Once turned on, she wouldn't know how to turn it off or even ask that it be turned off. For her, TV isn't entertaining but now dishes up a subtle form of suffering.

Even magazines have become menacing. Everything on the pages has equal weight. Ads, so much more emotive and colorful than gray paragraphs of text, draw her eye. I notice how many ads aimed at seniors show distressing pictures. She can't understand the headlines, but she feels the fear. The magazine falls in her lap, and she looks at me with worry.

Dad brings her a wildlife photography magazine. She flips through captivating pictures of birds and flowers and mountain goats then stops, transfixed, on a photo of a grizzly bear. She looks at the window. *Is it secure? Could a bear get in?* She can't turn the page to the butter-flies and chipmunks that follow. The bear grips her mind. I take that magazine back home.

104

Her room looks out on a meandering section of the narrow river that runs by the nursing home. We're told that moose have been spotted, though whitetail deer are more frequent. Canada geese and mallard ducks land in a bend where cattails grow. The view is a selling point.

On a half-frozen day, a deer falls through the ice. Another doe paces at the edge. The deer's front legs scrabble the lip of the ice but can't gain a footing. The struggle goes on. It's something that happens in the wild. And today it's happening slowly.

I step into the hall and ask a nurse if there's anything to be done. She says someone's called a game warden, but we both know there's no rescue on the way. The warden takes awhile to show up. If the deer drowns, they won't have to shoot it while residents locked in their own life struggles look on.

105

I come home, change my coat, grab a flashlight, and head out in the deepening twilight to walk the labyrinth. Afterward, I sit on the stone by the gate. The quiet is deep. I need this blankness of mind to offset a landscape teeming with need. Animals, two-legged and four-legged, forage, suffer, or sleep. I watch the stars appear and disappear as clouds move from west to east.

106

A new concern: Her bowels have no rhythm. This is no small thing. I learn that elderly folks can die from backed up stool that puts too much pressure on the vagus nerve.

The hospice nurses had time for close attention and found a routine. Now, Mom's on industrial time. She's got to perform, preferably on the aides' schedule. Her answer is to pucker up every hole—top and bottom—in disapproval.

Warm prune juice. Milk of magnesia. Now a fiber powder in water, which works too well and brings on diarrhea. Nothing works except a suppository every fourth day. Lying on the bed, aides chatting pleasantly over the clean-up and change of clothes, she closes her eyes. She is somewhere else—anywhere else.

What does the good life come down to? One new answer: Having a regular bowel movement that doesn't shred one's dignity or threaten one's life. We have work to do to get there.

107

Several rhythms overlap and clash here. Because Mom can't dress herself or eat on her own, she has to swim along in the daily routine of everyone else on her wing. No sleeping in, as she always liked to do. Her toileting, for the length of her stay here, will never cooperate.

Dad has his preference for visiting times. His routine matters, too.

The invoices come like clockwork.

I struggle to sense what will please her and be possible within the confines of each day. There's always a full schedule of activities, but mostly they slide by because she's busy napping, toileting, or visiting with Dad. That's okay. As much as the stimulation of activities helps, encountering so many people—*who are all these people?*—is also bewildering.

Christmas comes and goes. I bring homemade rice pudding, her Swedish mother's Christmas Eve tradition. She's not interested.

108

Many days she thinks she's living in a school. She knows her way around school. She knows how to do school.

She doesn't understand why the other teachers won't talk to her about their classes. She doesn't understand why she's sleeping at school. But believing this is school makes sense of the institutional feel of the place, the echoing sounds and voices in the hallway, and the group dining, though she wonders if there's enough food for the students given all the adults who eat here.

She's living inside her memory of school. It's a structure that makes sense out of this alien nonsense. And why not? She was an excellent teacher, with an uncommon talent for teaching kids how to read. She didn't brag about it, but I see now how deeply she inhabited this accomplishment, persisting years after her last day in a classroom.

In fact, her mother-self has largely disappeared while her teacher-self endures. Having four kids and raising them might seem to be unforgettable, but all that's gone now. Meanwhile, being a teacher still gives form to hazy days.

109

She's annoyed by the nurses who've laid her on her bed to inspect a spot on her tailbone, discussing it over her while laughing and trading thrift store shopping tips. They finally pull up her pants and address her: Does she want to be moved back to her chair?

Icily, she says, "I don't know. I'm just a piece of furniture."

The nurses laugh, but I hear the rebuke. True, she has dementia. She wears adult diapers. She can no longer bear her own weight. But she is still aware, at least sometimes, that her dignity is the first casualty in the understaffed, overburdened grind of the staff's to-do lists. It's a business model for manufacturing cars, not caring for vulnerable elders.

110

The aides' random clothes selections make Mom look like a picture made from several jigsaw puzzles. She looks down and doesn't recognize herself. Another definition of dignity: Wearing what reflects your own taste rather than being a doll for someone else's. I select outfits in color combinations she would choose and put them on hangers in her wardrobe.

I put up a sign that lets caregivers know that I do Mom's laundry. But they don't always read signs, and Mom's clothes start to go missing. An aide takes me to the room off the laundry with racks of clothes that haven't found their way back to their owners. This massive closet of orphans, despite each resident's initials written into every item on the first day they arrive.

I ask the aide why Mom's clothes landed in laundry limbo, when they're all clearly marked. He asks how her initials were written. Last initial first, I tell him. That's how the aide wielding the marker did it.

"Ah," he says. "It should've been first initial first." That's why the laundry people don't realize where they belong. One small miscommunication, multiplied over dozens of residents, with hundreds of consequences.

111

I arrive to find her cringing in her wheelchair next to a wall panel blaring an alarm while aides walk by. I arrive to find her sitting in her recliner, pants filled with diarrhea. Her glasses are broken by another resident, twice. Her clothes go missing again.

Aides put her hair up in tight braids. I can see by her expression that Mom hates it. Braids are for little girls, and she can't run her fingers through her hair, something she does to soothe herself. I take the braids out, and the aides aren't happy. I tell them I'll get her a haircut.

Oxygen tanks are regularly delivered to her room. She's never been on oxygen. I tell the nurse again about the misdelivery and make a note to check that we're not billed for it.

Staff have taken Mom's handmade quilt into the industrial laundry and now it's lost. I ask everyone to keep an eye out for it. The big name tag on the back will identify it.

A new resident next door to the south has a proximity alarm on his wheelchair, which goes off if he stands up. We know better than anyone how many (many) times he does. Mom thinks it's a fire alarm. "Should we evacuate? Is someone getting the students out?"

She picks at her pant leg, a sign that she needs the toilet, so I press the call button. We're patient. I'm not allowed to help her with toileting, so we wait. And wait. I go to the nurse's station to track down an aide. They're all busy, but we're on the list. The response time in the sales pitch is not the response time on the ground. The resident next door to the north has her own solution. She screams "HEEEEEELP!" at the top of her lungs until someone comes. It's unnerving but effective.

112

I talk to the nurses and social worker about ways to smooth things out, walking a fine line between offering solutions and being a nuisance. Any single thing is forgivable, but the new-thing-every-day wears thin. I tell them I can see how hard everyone's working. I know everyone means well. Nevertheless, my job is to advocate for Mom. That means, increasingly, I'm a nuisance, while repeating: *I see how hard everyone's working, and I appreciate your efforts.*

We find small tweaks, but Mom's just not a fit for this style of factory care. The people who do best here can speak up for themselves, using a call button or yelling for attention. In daily practice, there isn't a realistic amount of time for any given care activity. The aides are running off their feet, and I can see why burnout is a problem in the profession.

Most days I come home seething. I sigh a lot, cry in the car to shed frustration, remind myself, again and again, that the aides and staff are doing their best. And then I text Ali, the owner and primary caregiver at West Hills, to say hello and ask if she has an opening yet.

113

While the institution falters, individuals deliver what saving grace is to be had. One aide makes sure Mom is wheeled to a live concert happening down the hall. The activities director gets Mom to the watercolor painting session and the Valentine's Day sugar cookie decorating. Dad will look at that cookie for days before eating it.

Another aide puts a Fred Astaire song on the CD player while she dresses Mom each morning. Mom recalls that Fred Astaire's sister has the same name she does—Adele. Mom sings along, *Heaven... I'm in heaven... and my heart beats hmm hmm hmm hmm hmm hmm hmmmmm... and I seem to find the happiness I seek...* She even stiffens herself to help with the transfer from bed to wheelchair.

114

Mom's room is on the short leg of an L-shaped hallway. At the end, a locked door leads to the memory care wing, the secure part for people with dementia who may wander. Mom's immobility means that she's not required to be there. Small mercies.

The door has a square glass window at eye level. Sometimes I see a woman there, waiting for anyone to come down the hall. She beckons and shouts, though I can't hear what she's saying through the glass. I imagine she's asking me to open the door.

115

The constant drip of small crises scatters my thoughts. I go looking for them in the labyrinth.

Walking after dark, I wonder about memorizing the circuits. With some effort, could I walk this with my eyes closed? I decide against it. That would imprint memory (a form of the past) on the present. That would turn a walk into a performance of knowledge. That's not why I come here.

That said, I've walked so often that I recognize combinations of left and right turns. I'm no longer impatient about how long it takes or surprised when it feels like a few short minutes. It feels ordinary, and I like that.

Tonight, I enter through the gate with respect but not overawe. Pagans sometimes planted a tree at the center of a labyrinth—a tree of life growing from the umbilical of the world. That's an awful lot of significance circulating. Too much. Right now, I feel this walk as familiar as time with an old friend.

116

The aim is clear, but the path is awash in shit.

Good intentions guarantee nothing.

Many once-in-a-lifetime choices. No chance to learn and do better next time. There is no next time.

Any decision can go sideways.

Some days my best is not nearly good enough. Suboptimal will have to be okay.

Perfection is a realm of the dead.

117

A few times, she calls me her daughter. But does she know that for herself or did she overhear a nurse describe me as such and is playing along? I can't tell if she knows Dad or is just playing *as if* because she enjoys the attention. She is his wife (maybe), and she is not his wife.

Dad and I both come home angry. Grief by another route.

This ongoing slog of small dissipations drags Dad into a gray place. From moment to moment, nothing can be assumed, nothing taken for granted. The fabric of sense rips deeper.

118

The every-day-ness of this melts time. Every morning. Every after-noon. I remind myself I chose to be here, though I couldn't imagine this marathon.

Marathon? an inner voice says. *It's only been a few months.*

I eke out my energy to get myself in the car every morning and afternoon. To pick up Dad. To arrive and enter into whatever I find with Mom. Usually helping to get her onto the bedside commode or the toilet or having her brief changed. Identifying for her the sounds from the hallway. Flagging down the snack cart that won't stop because she can't ask. Listening for clues about where she thinks she is or what she needs.

I can't see beyond this. Every extra thought comes with a cost, and every cost feels too high.

I walk. I call a friend. I write a letter. I remind myself that the habits I build now are the ones that will be with me at the end. Do I want the habit of despair to be my last thought? An ugly prospect.

119

The world beyond has faded, except for the boldest headlines. COVID-19 at first feels far away. Then Washington state reports outbreaks in nursing homes. I sit up.

I keep a shoulder bag packed with copies of legal paperwork, notebook, reading glasses, a change of clothes, bottle of water, phone charger... ready to go. I don't know what's to come, but whatever it is, I'll need to be ready.

I'm always on standby. My mind skates the surface. I can't quite let myself get lost in any task. Nothing that can't be dropped in an instant for that higher priority. No room for flow.

Is this how firefighters in the firehouse feel?

120

I drive Dad home from visiting Mom. Make him lunch, then he goes upstairs for his usual afternoon nap. He says he sometimes feels her in bed with him, feels her foot running up his calf.

I go outside to find the cat. Dad says petting the cat is good for my blood pressure. The cat doesn't care how I feel. She's interested in routines and moments. I sit in the doorway of the old milking barn, and she emerges from tall grass just beyond the corral fence. Her attention is keen and relaxed, all at once. I admire that.

She sits on my lap, but she doesn't like to be held. She was born wild and likes company on her own terms. I pet her until something catches her eye in the haystack, and she's gone. She doesn't look back. She's all forward trajectory, calculating speed and distance to her objective: the rustle of prey or a place safer than wherever she is now.

I walk up the dry irrigation ditch, throwing downed tree limbs onto the bank. The top of the bank is about waist high, and it feels right to be walking below ground in this subterranean mood. The cat shows up and walks alongside me, ambling, disinterested. Then, without warning, she veers sideways into dried leaves, emerges with jaws full of furry vole.

I keep moving up the ditch. She drops the vole, lets it drag itself a few inches, puts a paw on it, feels it struggle, bites it again with a killing crunch. She doesn't lack skill. And with voles' reproduction rates, she'll never lack for a meal.

121

Should we try a rehab routine to strengthen Mom's arms and upper body? It would make transfers to and from the bed and wheelchair easier and safer. The physical therapist stops by with exercise bands and a sheaf of drawings and instructions.

Mom follows along, politely nodding and mirroring the motions. She humors the therapist, but on following days she's not about to humor me. I try to make it a game. She's not fooled. She was never one for exercise, and she's not about to start now.

Her strength is what it is. She will always need help getting from bed to chair, from chair to toilet. But even this modest bit of change in position will be enough to hold off pressure sores and skin breakdown so typical in her situation.

She doesn't like the lifts, hoists, and hugs that it takes to move her. Sometimes politeness motivates her to help. But more often, she's annoyed at being shifted and goes limp, turning herself into dead-weight, a loose sack of sand. All this without comment or complaint but certainly with an unmistakable message.

122

When everything aligns, the moment Mom needs the toilet is the moment there are people to help her get there. It's rare. That exercise is no longer a peaceful, long meditation in the blue bathroom upstairs. Safety and speed override privacy now. Every act is a public act. Everyone is on the clock, and the faster it all comes out the better. Dignity is collateral damage.

The choreography of lifting, holding-while-cleaning, and moving from wheelchair to toilet requires two people. I'm in a position to help, though an aide says I don't need to if I'd rather not. She says many kids don't want that view of their parent's body. I wipe Mom clean and think later about how many times she wiped my bottom without complaint.

123

Is this too much about bowel movements and adult briefs and poop and pee and generalized shit? It's not what I want to talk about in relation to my mother. It's not dignified.

The sanitized terms "bowel care" and "toileting" make it sound routine, which—when things are going well—it is. It's the welcome sign of a body doing its work.

But she's never found a routine here. She doesn't even understand why she has to go through this disruptive exercise. "Why does it keep happening? Where does it come from?" she wants to know. I tell her that the food she eats is digested inside to take out the nutrients, and what's left over comes out her behind. But that doesn't make sense to her, because she doesn't remember eating, though her appetite's good these days.

As for the metaphorical shit that comes her way, I, too, feel blank. Why does it keep happening? Some days it's easier to shrug and go along with whatever's unfolding. Forget about questioning the opaque cause-and-effect. Even in an institution this size, the sense of responsibility is dispersed. Everyone is doing their best, so why does so much go wrong? *Why does the shit keep happening?*

The minimal hopes I had for Mom's comfort in this well-meaning but ill-fitting place have vanished. The vase next to the framed picture of her mother needs fresh flowers. I text Ali. Is a room available yet at West Hills?

124

I get along with this post-stroke woman so much better than I got along with the mother who, around me, was buttoned-up and tongue-tied, never able to talk about the difficult things we shared. Sometimes we just sit together, leaving space for a thought that may take long minutes to find its way to the throat.

Denial was her superpower, constructive for her but destructive for me. In the end, it may be the secret to her endurance. I can see a throughline from the way she patiently withstood her husband's military absences to the way she now withstands whatever wedges itself between sunrises over the old mountains and sunsets over the newer mountains, the valley of days in between—whether sunny, snowy, gray, or blue skied—each and every one she declares "a good day."

125

Mom can no longer follow a narrative thread, but that doesn't mean she no longer enjoys books. She sits rapt listening to me read favorite stories or poems aloud. She isn't following the beginning-middle-end, but something in the characters or sounds rings for her. An echo of pleasure makes her smile.

When I read a poem she read to decades of her young students, she leans forward and, with relish, chimes in with the catchy rhymes at the end of lines. Then leans back, tears on her cheeks from the leaping joy of sounds that are friends, reaching through fog to speak to her.

Sometimes, when I'm in the middle of reading a poem, she reaches over and turns the page, as a child would, not in response to anything but her own sense that this is what we do with books. We turn the page. And so we do.

126

Lessons are everywhere, if I can scrape together the focus to find them. I learn new skills, new terms, new ideas, new habits of mind. I try to empathize with the difficult tasks everyone has, including and especially Mom. Otherwise, I'll fail to do the best I could. I'll hurt the situation rather than help. I'll confuse care with control. I'll confuse grief with grievance.

She is here and not here. I grieve the person who no longer recognizes me while loving the person who is here—who is, in fact, emerging. She echoes herself, and the self she is today is always the authentic one.

Sadness drips through me, but around her I stay cheerful. I watch for gestures that are tacit requests for understanding. And because we have history, I can guess better than most what she means. This is what I can bring to this messy table.

I let go (again and again) the woman who was. I don't insist that she be my mother. Something new is happening. I don't need to replay the relationship that defined us for decades. Nostalgia is a way of cursing the present.

127

"What's on your mind?" I ask.

"I'm thinking about how calm I am when you're here." Being here matters.

Later, she sees my name on a contact information sign taped to her wall. "That's my daughter's name," she tells me. "I didn't know she was involved in all this."

128

I see Les down by the barn. His dog Sammy runs at me, a reliably excited greeting, no matter what my mood. He asks if I saw the elk tracks in the snow by the driveway entrance. A small herd came through to check the fence around his haystack.

Les and I have both been by that spot twice today. Nope, I didn't see the tracks. My eye isn't tuned to this landscape. There's no way to calculate how much I don't see. How do you measure the scope of what goes unnoticed?

My eye is tuned to the traces in Mom's behavior and mood. *What does she want that she's not asking for? What activity might divert her when she's anxious? What idea is yet to be considered? What have I missed?*

129

Persistence, luck, and good timing. A room opens up at West Hills, our first choice of assisted living care. Mom is wheeled through the front door, looks around, and declares that it feels like home.

Her room on the ground floor of the two-story log house is reliably quiet. No rattling metal carts in the background. No proximity alarms or TV noises through the wall. We've outfitted the room with bedside table, power-lift recliner, and bookshelves to hold framed pictures, flower vases, and elaborate pop-up cards her teacher friends send. A bulletin board holds a calendar for care notes, family photos, and medical contact details. Dad relaxes and looks forward to visiting.

We get to know the three other first-floor ladies. At the common dining table, one holds Mom's hand and tells her how pretty she is. They have juice and cookies together. They will paint pictures, have manicures, and watch movies of babies and puppies. This is the sweet female companionship Mom's been wanting nearby for years.

Ali, a warmhearted dynamo always ready with a hug, is the main caregiver and one half of the couple that owns West Hills. Ali is short for Alina, which she tells us means "comfort" in her native Romanian.

She somehow balances the professional and personal with a genuine interest in each resident's particularity. She asks what Mom does and doesn't like to eat, to wear, to do… she wants Mom to have whatever will make her happy. Mom says she always wanted a sister. Ali comes from a big family and readily says she'll be Mom's "little sister." Mom lights up and later cries heartfelt, happy tears when Ali tucks her in and kisses her "big sister" on the cheek.

130

Mom once again has homecooked food in a relaxed setting that feels like eating with a family. No more institutional fare, pureed and plopped into separate unidentifiable piles. No more rush to meals in a cafeteria with dozens of other people who never look her in the eye.

Ali plies her with favorite foods, and I stock the cupboards with enough snacks for everyone. There's space for Dad's favorite coffee, too, so he feels more at home when we visit. Ali tells us she's never heard his name before—Harold—but remembers it by thinking of the carol lyric: *Hark the herald angels sing...*

It's a cheerful atmosphere. Loving. It feels *normal,* and now I know how extraordinary that is for an eldercare setting.

131

A few weeks later, COVID-19 makes its way to Montana. Statewide restrictions end our visits inside the house. After the initial panic eases, we visit Mom at her glass French doors that connect to a porch.

Inside, Ali wheels Mom's chair close to the glass. Outside, I pull Dad's chair up. They place their palms on opposite sides of the pane, a touch through the barrier. She doesn't understand why we don't come in.

132

Weeks go by, and after an enjoyable day with the other ladies preparing for Easter, Mom goes to bed and will not want to get up again.

She's not in any pain. She barely speaks. She doesn't want to eat. There's no obvious injury, but Ali recognizes signs in her behavior. She's had another stroke.

We reactivate hospice. No graduation this time.

133

Will hospice nurses be allowed to care for Mom? The strictest rules for licensed nursing homes, such as she just came from, have confined residents to their rooms and barred all outsiders, including hospice workers, from entering.

But the guidance for small assisted living facilities has a little more leeway to customize a response. Mom's room, fortuitously, can be quarantined from the rest of the house by closing the door to the common area and using the French doors as entrance and exit. Ali's teenage daughters sometimes helped with Mom's care, but now Ali becomes her sole caregiver.

With precautions of masks, gloves, and antiseptic cleaning routines, hospice nurses will be able to come and go. Dad and I will be allowed limited visits in the room under compassionate exemption rules. This will be our luckiest of breaks.

134

Days pass, and she rests comfortably. She's on a minimal dose of morphine to aid her breathing. When Dad sits by her bed, talking quietly to her, holding her hand, she floats up with a faint smile, sometimes returning a gentle pressure on his hand.

We've had the siblings in her ear by phone, but there's no question of another gathering at her bedside. That earlier goodbye will have to comfort them now.

135

Hold the hand of someone who's dying and it becomes blindingly clear: there's nowhere to run. The trivial wriggles away. The busy-for-busy's-sake huffs absurdly. Efficiency becomes a ridiculous, even hurtful, measure for what's occurring.

Every vulnerability is being dug up in this wild and jagged slide from dementia to stroke to last breath. I've placed myself on this path. The way I hold myself through it will be an accomplishment all its own.

My aim reverses again. I focus on enabling her dignified and comfortable exit, to clear the way to a good death.

136

A friend asks what I mean by a "good death." I lean on my experience with Florence, her passage marked by a warm solemnity and comfort—and something more that emerged from having sufficient time and support to resolve what wanted resolving.

Yes, to reminisce about what won't let go. Yes, to experience what's been missing, like a certain kind of companionship. Yes, to satisfy a lingering appetite. Yes, to feel cleansed after a sponge bath by caring hands.

Yes to those things, but also *yes* to requests that seemed strange, like Florence asking me to walk with her, embracing each other as if we were dancing a tango, toward an invisible narrow door that she said she had to get through.

Yes, when she urgently wanted me to clear off the windowsill and refrigerator, leaving uncluttered white space for her to gaze on.

Yes, when she wanted to be laid on the floor on her back, wondering what it might be like to be a body in a grave.

Yes to that unpredictable something more—whatever it is—that becomes possible in a neutral space of no judgment. The self accomplishing itself, a culmination and affirmation of a person's uniqueness, as free as one can ever be from our histories' limitations.

137

Later, Les will show me how to tell whether a fencepost is rotten by tapping a hammer on it and listening to the sound it makes. He'll help me sort through a stack of planks that, despite being propped up off the ground, has for decades been rotting from the bottom up.

I'll tell him about the time, decades ago, that Dad asked Mom and me to help him pull a plank from near the bottom of that pile. He figured if he had an extra pair of hands, he could slip that plank out without moving all the ones above it. I didn't understand how he was going to get it done, but he clearly had a plan.

We stood by, waiting for him to direct us.

"Well, come on!"

Mom and I looked at each other. "What do you want us to do?"

He snorted a little—*wasn't it obvious?*—then gave a few rough directions until I understood, and we got the plank.

Mom said out of the corner of her mouth, "He would've been a lousy teacher."

I agreed, only to find out later from unearthed military reports that in fact he had been an excellent in-flight navigation instructor, flexible and generous with his students. So why did he become so taciturn with us on the ranch? Why did we have to drag instructions out of him? Why did he expect us to read his mind?

Was this Dad's version of what Mom would sometimes say to me, with an unnameable expression: "If you love me, you'll know what I mean."

It's a rotten premise that took years to unpick, but as a kid it kept me trained closely on her for every clue that might reveal what went unspoken—dedicated attention that proved how much I loved her. And though she never intended it, that practice now gives me more than average ability to divine meaning from her smallest gesture, now that communication comes in the lift of an eyebrow or a whisper.

138

She is still with us, breaking every rough expectation about the when of active dying. How many times has she rallied? We brace for each day to be the last, and then she finds another way back.

This tenacity—after presenting herself all her life as physically fragile. That was what her mind believed, the story she told herself about herself, while her body was capable of much more.

I wonder about the stories I tell myself about myself. Do they help? Can I change the ones that hurt? The mental game is real.

<h1 style="text-align:center">139</h1>

Florence, too, broke every expectation of her hospice team. Her eyes flickered behind closed lids, while I wondered *what's keeping her here?*

Was Florence simply attached to her routine? Wake up. Walk. Read the paper. Comb hair. Eat breakfast. Read letters. Not an exciting routine, but *her* routine. Her idea about the afterlife was basically more of the same—just somewhere else.

Was Florence hanging on out of stubbornness? Was death simply a failure to live? The eternal laziness of a morning when she didn't have the energy to get out of bed and go walking? Unacceptable.

Two weeks into Florence's long goodbye, her palms grew dusky as circulation slowed. The skin on her feet creased, shrunken around tendons as her body slowly dehydrated. Her face was smooth, skin soft. A blue cast appeared around her mouth. Her hair—a thick, wavy white cloud—was still beautifully alive.

One wrist draped off the edge of the bed, elegantly casual. She was comfortable physically, but was she still struggling in other unseen ways? There was no way to know, but the fact that she was still here, days past anyone's expectation, pointed to something not ready to finish. Or maybe it was the sheer power of physicality, a heart born to beat that knows nothing else but to go on and on and on.

Was I holding her here? She could be very particular. Was she annoyed with me over some way that I hadn't cared for her exactly as she wanted? I had done my best, but I was learning on the job. I sat by her bedside and asked her forgiveness for any way I hadn't done right by her. She grimaced a little. Agreement or disagreement? Forgiveness or a brushing aside of a mistaken idea? No way to tell.

The next day, I talked with hospice staff and, at their suggestion, asked her to let *me* go. I cleaned the dried medication from her cheek, put balm on her lips, combed her hair, straightened the shawl over her, kissed her, and told her I wouldn't go back to my life until she found her new life. If she went, then I could go. We both needed to move out of terminal restlessness and find the next life. No response.

I noticed that Florence had one unpainted fingernail. The bright red nail polish on one forefinger had been stripped so that an oxygen sensor would read properly. Now there was no need to take vital signs. The center's beautician came to paint that lone undressed nail. Florence always did her best to present well and properly. Maybe she was just waiting for that?

I look at Mom, resting comfortably, and can't imagine what remains undone.

140

These beings don't care that Mom is dying: the whitetail deer and elk that move through the fields on their way to water, graze, or rest. The pairs of quail and their skittering broods. The cows and their small calves. The bulls grumbling and bellowing for the cows. The barn cat, peering down from the top of the haystack. The chickadees, nut hatches, downy woodpeckers, magpies, flickers, chimney swifts that will raise two broods in one summer, turkey vultures and bald eagles looking for a carcass to pick, and red-tailed hawk. The stray ewe and her twin lambs who escape from a farm to the east and find their way to our corral, the neighbor's horses, the other neighbor's chickens, the moose and bear that once wandered through and now wander in Dad's stories. Fire ants making mounds. Honeybees from the neighbor's hives. The occasional bumblebee. The robins will be late to show up in the spring.

141

She endures.

I feel something in my gut, dislodged from somewhere else, a soft fist expanding and dissolving all at once: a certainty—wholly irrational—when I see the lavender rings around her eyes, the pooling of blood that signals the end approaching—that *she could not possibly die.* MY MOTHER GOES ON FOREVER says that remnant of child in me, remnant of those early days when the world is still whole. Before reaching for apples and falling out of trees and breaking limbs. Before intellect, when knowledge is still something made in the flesh, in the trust before betrayal shows up in the other's face. That memory of oneness. That certainty that this moment is all there is, and it will go on forever.

I was not expecting that.

142

Hospice and Ali work well together, with obvious mutual respect. This is a relief. I know it can be otherwise.

To avoid disagreements over Florence's care, hospice was primary and gave instructions to the assisted living nurses. It worked well until one Saturday at 2:00 a.m., when a weekend nurse decided that Florence was resting nicely and didn't need her scheduled dose of morphine.

The nurse stood silhouetted in the open door, hall light flooding around her to cast a dim light on Florence's recliner, where she slept. I sat on the floor, back against the recliner, and whispered that we already discovered that waiting until she showed signs of needing the morphine caused a rollercoaster of distress. The nurse disagreed. I said it wasn't her decision to make. She pushed back: *in her medical opinion... with her medical responsibility...*

Just before I had to say, "So do you want to call hospice or do you want me to?" Florence roused and asked for the medication. I asked for a different nurse to support Florence the following night.

143

The double act I practice: To be here as fully as I can be, and at the same time quiet my own needs. *This is not about me.*

I'm in the room as someone who has legs and a reach that she may need. Fetch the water for the sponge that will drip relief into her dry cheek. Put balm on her papery lips. Adjust the window shade when the sun reaches that annoying angle.

Am I listening with more than ears? A small gesture in a failing body can speak volumes. The pace of breath. A brow calm or knitted. A hand loose on the sheets. A finger twitching. All ways of showing and telling.

What I'm doing is profoundly important to me though it's impossible to say exactly how or why. And saying exactly how or why is not necessary. The less I worry about myself, the more I see.

144

The neighbor's peacocks and peahens stroll across the road to roost in the trees along the irrigation ditch. They remind me of the peafowl that wander around the Hollywood Forever Cemetery, where two of Mom's aunts are buried in a double-decker gravesite. One of them had dementia. The other cared for her until the end.

I find long tail feathers in the grass, the distinctive eye looking skyward. One day I see the biggest peacock in the middle of his home pasture, tail fully fanned, displaying his magnificence to a couple of old horses. They stand a few feet away, curious, heads lowered to the peacock's eye level. An image as improbable as everything else that's happening.

145

How does one learn to leave?

To leave gracefully?

At the right moment, not prematurely out of misplaced priorities (the laundry can wait) or fear (I can bear whatever happens here)?

At the right moment, not dragging or having stayed too long?

I learn how to go.

Really go, ready to return (always the unexpected turn) while I watch this moment slide away.

The present is always sliding away into the past, that chuckling stream.

146

The gravity of the deathbed: as weightless as breath and as heavy as meat. There's still time for last surges of forgiveness, rage, and love. I sit near her bed thinking the range as fully and as honestly as I can manage, not touching her, at enough distance so as not to disturb her flesh.

The body in its frailty. The mind in its wandering.

Threads dissolving and gathering force, concentrated toward a single breath. After all enthusiasm and despair are spent, the last one. She floats on a surface unknowable to me.

I have silent talks with myself about our shared problems. I think of her ability to ignore and endure them in plain sight and of my need to uproot them. I think of the days we had together when my siblings were at school. What did I learn through that close time? Without distractions, did I see the shadows that dogged her and whistle them over to my side?

Sit.

Stay.

Lay down.

I sit at her bedside now half thinking our mundane history and wondering about the history I can't know—the deal we struck without words that took me away for most of our lives and brought me back for these last years.

Silence is so thick it feels solid. The tangibility is overwhelming.

147

A hospice nurse advises that we may see short, rapid breaths followed by a pause so long it seems like the end. Cheyne-Stokes breaths. *Is this her last? Is it?*

Deep inhale. No. That was the pause between a wave washing in to hug the sand and spread its foam… and washing out again. A ragged, ongoing sigh.

When we lived on Oahu, we took a vacation to Maui. We stayed in a beach bungalow, in a time before the beach disappeared under resorts and hotels. Mom told me that while the rest of us slept, she sat up in the dark listening to each wave wash in, holding her breath until she heard it wash out again. Any one of them could continue up the beach and flood the bungalow, perhaps wash us out into the deep. She didn't trust the ocean to behave.

148

Dad usually went to bed earlier than Mom. Before heading up the stairs to their bedroom, he'd kiss her and say, "I'll save you a place." It's their longstanding joke.

Now he holds her hand and says quietly, "Wherever you're going, save me a place."

149

A hospice nurse tells me that if Mom wants me in the room when she dies, I will be there. If not, I won't be. It's not up to me. She'll choose it.

Ali has attended many people through hospice. Her family lives in the back of the large house, but at this stage, Ali sleeps lightly in Mom's recliner or in a room across the hall, with Mom's room door open. At 1:30 a.m., Ali wakes from a short sleep for no particular reason. She goes to Mom's room, sees her take a few rapid breaths, a panting last sprint, and then stop. Really stop.

Ali stays with her quietly for some fifteen minutes, something I've asked her to do after hearing about the short period of electrical activity that continues in the brain after the heart stops. No one knows its significance, but whatever it is, we make space for it.

By 2:30 a.m., I'm there with Ali and a hospice nurse who's declared Mom's time of death. No need to call a coroner or sheriff. No circus. We quietly dress Mom in one of her favorite outfits with a floral jacket that reminds us of spring. I comb her hair.

Ali and the nurse leave me to sit with her. I think about going to the ranch now, but what's the point of getting Dad out of bed in the dark? Let him wake up one more time with her in the world.

Her body cools. When the sun breaks over the eastern ridge, I go to the ranch. Dad will be up. He'll have dressed, made a pot of coffee, let the dog out, fetched the paper, and checked the weather forecast.

Does he want to see her? Yes. So we go to her. He says she looks elegant. We leave before the hearse arrives to collect her cold body.

Carry On

150

I'm relieved that her anxiety and bewilderment are done.

151

In the hay barn are a couple dozen feedsacks filled with pinecones collected for starting fires in the wood stove. They're draped in years of cobwebs and dust. Wasps have built a nest at the intersection where two sacks lean against each other, an elaborate multilevel construction the size of my head. I ask Dad if I can put those bags on the burn pile.

No.

Later I realize that these are the last pinecones Mom collected. It was one of her usual tasks through the summer and fall. Sometimes she and Dad did it together.

These sacks, moldering in the barn's dusk, sun filtered in vertical slices through gaps in the weathered boards, are evidence of her intention and will, when she still had intention and will. A store of her plans and work for their shared future.

152

The lid jumps on the rice cooker. Soon I'll make baked rice pudding from the recipe Mom cooked. Her mother's recipe, learned from her mother, a bitter, sneaky woman who drove her husband off their Minnesota farm. He died when he fell through an upper floor railing in a poorhouse by the Mississippi River.

The story goes that this Swedish great-grandmother sent her daughter into the farmyard during a storm, holding a tin cup of grain to feed chickens. That girl was struck by lightning, a tragedy that was, in fact, dumb luck. She walked with a sister to the nearest town that had a doctor, where the sister left her to recover.

She did. Instead of returning to the farm, she stayed on with the doctor's family, got a high school diploma, then moved to Minneapolis to become a telegrapher with Western Union. She was so fast at Morse code that her telegraph key was modified to keep up with her speed. She became a teacher in the telegraphy school, where she met the man who failed the course but became her husband. They had two children, my mother the younger, named after one of her mother's telegrapher friends.

This story survives. Even the sneaky, bitter ancestor still has a hand in things, thanks to the delicious recipe she brought with her from the Old Country. I make it for Dad, who's lost his wife of 65 years, 8 months, and 22 days.

153

Does grief change us? Or does it refine us, making us more obviously who we were all along?

154

For about a week after she died, I see, out of the corner of my eye, a figure like a small bird flying at eye level. When I turn to look, it's gone. Flesh beyond the perception of eyes. This phantom accompanies me.

155

A labyrinth's ancient architecture is sufficient unto itself, winding from the direction of sunrise and back again. Now, spring warms the occasional walkers, who show up at any time of the month but especially around a full or new moon. For me, this is the season of weeding and pruning, not walking.

I think of this labyrinth's designer, Patty, who calmed her mind in these circuits. I, too, feel my inner chatter settle into something more like dialogue. Her husband Helmut has told me of her difficult death, painful despite his best efforts to make it less so. She didn't want his help and wouldn't have it. A stark reminder that this labyrinth is solace, but it's not a solution.

I walk within shapes Patty left behind, vaguely aware of how things can go wrong, despite best and loving efforts. Most things are not like this labyrinth, with its single path to the center and no choices along the way but to attend to the next step. And I wonder why, on some days, even that single path feels like walking a tightrope?

156

COVID restrictions preclude any thought of a memorial service or funeral. A relief, really, for this fractured family. I take no comfort in togetherness, and Dad hates funerals. As a boy growing up in a rural churchgoing family, he was brought along to every goodbye. He says he was tired of funerals by the time he was six.

Which isn't to say we don't mourn, but Dad's stoicism is our cue. This won't be helpful for some of us. Grief with nowhere to land can detonate. All the ways we don't communicate will intrude and resound as background interference.

Mom's cremated, and her ashes sit in a velveteen bag on her piano. Next to the bag is a framed picture of her from college, looking eager and poised for whatever would come next.

157

A friend calls. Across 2,000 miles our conversation wanders, breathing generosities and trust. Long distance relationships have their limitations, but when physical presence is impossible, a sort of projected presence, mindful and ineffable, has to do.

I learned that early. Dad was so often away. To keep his disappearances from being total, we wrote letters, sent chocolate chip cookies in metal coffee tins, made reel-to-reel tapes, put pins on maps to locate him, imagined conversations (longing ones and angry ones—distance has its price). In those days of long waits between mail deliveries and no thought of expensive overseas phone calls, I learned to sustain him in my mind. Never mind that it didn't match the man who returned from the tropics. I believed.

Now, belief and knowing flex together like a small animal in me, warmed by the effort to listen and the pleasure of being heard. For weeks, sentences have been lobbed *at* me. Now my friend and I speak *to* and *with*. Somewhere in our stew of dark jokes and what-if's we pay attention. We appear to each other.

158

Were Mom's repetitive thoughts a glitch in her deteriorating matrix or a story demanding to be told? Maybe both?

The repetition of grief over her mother's death, fresh every time. The tearful demand to go home to her teenage house. The paranoia over lurking dangers with details sprung from those same early years. The concern over not mistaking the fake for the real.

So much of herself was lost, and she seemed to follow what remained in circles, finding kinder thoughts of her mother, father, brother, and (I venture) herself. Did she lay the painful repetitions to rest or were they simply forgotten? Ghosts gone not because she said goodbye but because the neurons on which they traveled failed to deliver their cruel message?

Did I hear what wanted to be heard? Did I meet the gaze that wanted to be met? I repeat circular thoughts until some leap breaks in with a way out of the trap. Repetition is a question in search of an answer. If no answer is possible, then a new frame and a kinder horizon must do.

159

COVID-19 deaths mount, and there's no recognition. A few months into the pandemic, I calculate that if we were to stop for one second for each of the dead in the U.S., we'd be still for more than 37 hours.

But there's no call to mourn together, to feel our capacity to hold this weight under which any one of us, on any given day, may collapse. And in not mourning, we take in and breathe out a subtle message: *those lives aren't grievable.*

The amount of pain circulating is unfathomable. People are hurt and scared, and anger steps in where empathy might have been. It's insane to run so hard from death. Avoiding mourning is a way of avoiding life, the thing at the root, where mourning has been a silent companion all along.

My loved one is dead, and the world we shared is gone. How do I go on?

Does anyone see my pain? Does anyone share it?

Who am I now that I'm not held in that embrace?

Who will say my name?

This essential disturbance breaks brains, raises fortresses, and births apocalyptic visions. One by one, we work on repair. Collectively, we convulse.

160

Dad and I have to find a new rhythm. The driving force is gone. The organizing center of the routine has vanished. We need new reasons to focus.

That's not so hard at this time of year when there's so much to do outside. The snow is gone, and the ground is coming back to life. There will be rhubarb to water. Mom's bulb garden to weed. Irrigation ditches to clean. Dead limbs to pick up out of the hayfields. Burn piles to light and tend...

And the paperwork that arrives with a person's death. Phone calls, emails, forms, followups... Dad doesn't have the patience for it, and his shaky handwriting and dimming eyesight make it difficult. I run it all by him. He nods and waves me on my way.

We take her name off of financial accounts, the ranch property, and vehicle titles. We change beneficiary designations on Dad's accounts. She was always his heir. They shared everything except her teacher's retirement account. That was supposed to support her after he was gone. They never imagined that he would outlive her.

161

Routine pushes forward even when we can't. Get up. Check the temperature outside. Get the dog up and let her out. Make coffee. Get the paper. Check the forecast. Read the sports page. Work through the bridge column.

What's on the morning agenda? Maybe a visit with Les. *How're the calves and cows doing? How're the fields looking? How's irrigation going? Is all the equipment ready for haying?* Over lunch we talk about Mom, details that remain to be settled, and how well hospice and Ali cared for her.

His tremor, which affects his balance, is noticeably worse. He doesn't want to talk about it. Doesn't want to see his doctor about it. At times, I see him stagger in a sudden loss of balance. Les sees it, too. Dad, so far, rights himself with his walking stick.

162

Dad can grumble out a tale or three of times he was wronged, all the way back to childhood. Some are small. He might chuckle over those. Others are no laughing matter.

Every time he rehearses one of those stories, I see his body straighten up in righteous indignation. Is it my imagination, or does he fall into this more often now? Does recalling things that make him angry counteract the downward pull of grief? Is it self-medication against despair or depression, states not allowed in his world?

The stories seem to lift him up. It's an emotional sleight-of-hand that puts everything and everyone in their place, with him head of the table.

163

Dad drives a tractor dragging a harrow over the fields, breaking up months of cow pies. A few months later, the harrow is switched for an 8-foot mower arm with spinning blades to cut hay.

Les will make the first pass around the field's perimeter, leaving a visible line that's easier for Dad to see and follow. Dad will have some things to say about how Les opens a field. *Not the way he'd do it.* And after wearing out his irritation over clockwise or counterclockwise and what has no effect on the outcome of the hay, he concedes that, though Les is younger, Les has been making hay for more years than he has.

164

In the summer heat, Lady uncharacteristically follows Dad to the far field when he drives the tractor out to mow hay. Entranced by the smell of mice in the downed grass, she can't hear the spinning blades nearing her hindquarters, and Dad (also mostly deaf) can't turn to see that she's there.

I run for her and afterward, uninjured, she looks at me perplexed. I lead her back along the cut field edge, unfamiliar now that all the usual trail smells are obliterated. She follows me and picks up the undisturbed scent at the gate to the next field. She goes on alone along the fence, back to the house.

I sit on a large rock and watch Dad make rounds, hailing each other every time he passes. The heat and humidity in the bottom of the field are brutal. A couple hours later, the mowing isn't done, but he agrees to drive back to the house. He parks under a pine tree and stumbles off the tractor, delirious. He says he had a vivid image of Mom when they were first courting, young and with everything ahead of them. He's sure that a lone tree across the field was a person waving at him.

What must it be like, I wonder, to now be without the body that has been with you for three-quarters of your life? He's mourned her, drop by drop, over the course of her dementia, but the complete absence of her body is something else.

165

We're having tomato soup for lunch, and I've put out saltine crackers. Wrong. Tomato soup requires Townhouse crackers. Saltines are for a standalone snack. Club crackers go with chili.

It would be easy to see this as arbitrary whim. *Is he winding me up? Reminding me who's boss?* This could be the stuff of petty household drama. *You want different crackers? Get 'em yourself.*

But these cracker preferences are long-held. I don't remember so many varieties growing up. Finances were tighter then. The expansion of the cracker menu is a small sign of prosperity. He's worked hard to have the different cracker combinations that he likes best.

I put the saltines back in the cupboard and put out a sleeve of oblong Townhouse crackers. Conferring dignity, in daily practice, comes down to respect for the other's particularity, no rationale or understanding required. Dignity is asking for three different kinds of crackers and getting them, without argument or complaint.

166

A rule of thumb in screenwriting is that the main character must be in every scene, physically present or invoked in conversation among the other characters. The main character is the one on everyone's mind, the one everyone's attention returns to, no matter what.

By this standard, Mom is the main character in the family, even in death. Even Dad is a supporting player. Some days we take a longer way around, but talk always draws back to her. Iron filings to a magnet.

167

Mom, then in her late 70s, told me that when she was a teenager she had written some stories that were published. She'd never mentioned such a thing to anyone else, as far as I knew. She didn't say more but gave me a few issues of the small magazine, founded and run by a teenager in West Virginia during the 1940s. I saw Mom's name in the masthead, but none of the issues contained any of her writing. Now, going through stashes for needed paperwork, I find a second envelope with more issues. I know what I'm looking for.

The half dozen pieces she wrote are all strikingly different in genre and tone. She was experimenting. One is pure patriotism, not surprising in the early 1940s. Another is shyly romantic. The most dramatic story is about a teenager stuck caring for a tyrannical old aunt. The young woman, to get out of the trap, feeds her aunt poison. But the aunt is too knowing, and as she dies lays something of a curse: *I know it was you. You'll never be free of me. You'll feel guilty the rest of your life.* The young woman, however, will have the last unspoken word. Cheerfully defiant, she walks into the ocean.

Mom had kept these hidden issues for more than fifty years, carrying them through six household moves. The stories were clearly important to her, but why was she so secretive about them? Too bold? Too revealing? Not in keeping with her well-ordered life as wife and mother?

I would've appreciated knowing that author. Where was she all my life?

168

An elderly neighbor dies. Dad asks me to buy flowers and says in so many words that it'd be nice if I went to the funeral at the small white church in the center of town, to represent the family. I dig out clothes I last wore to a business meeting in Santa Barbara, simple but respectful.

I'm woefully overdressed. Clearly not from here. I should've started with a clean pair of jeans and good cowboy boots. Inside the church, it's strange to see the men with no hats—trucker or cowboy. I never noticed that I only see them outside, under hats.

The youngest son, who took care of his mother in her last years, tells a story about the two of them chased by a bull across a field and up a tree. Afterward, I half listen to the preacher do fire and brimstone while I wonder what I'd say, if given one story to tell about different people I know.

169

Dad didn't want a funeral, but I feel a vacuum where some point of mourning should be. I ask the siblings to send me something they'd want in a memorial book. Predictably, we write about four different mothers. I put those together with images from her scrapbooks and photos from the span of her life. A portrait. I write this:

~

The mother does the dishes. By conservative estimate, Mom washed dishes more than 35,000 times in her married life. I can't remember her ever saying that she enjoyed doing dishes (other than the warmth of the water on a chilly day), but she let us take that impression away when she shooed us out of the kitchen with that signature phrase. Her tone could end any argument before it even began: *The mother does the dishes.*

If we were allowed to help, it was only to dry, maybe on a holiday when pans and plates piled up too high for a single drying rack. In Rapid City, Uncle Bill marveled at what a tower she could construct of all the bowls and cups. He remembers her finishing the washing, pulling the plug, and walking away without a backward glance at whatever was left after water drained and suds faded. I imagine her having a moment of satisfaction, like Sisyphus with his rock at the top of the hill, enjoying one sigh of accomplishment before it started all over again.

She never seemed to want an automatic dishwasher. The one in Grand Forks that leaked was never repaired. The one in the ranch house was removed (or maybe never installed?) to make more cupboard space. There were always reasons, but they all amounted to her signing up for a several-times-a-day dose of what sure looked like drudgery.

Even as dementia eroded her attention for daily tasks, she held fiercely to her ownership of doing those dishes. That was unshakably her thing, even as dishes piled up over days. She would bristle if I began to run a sink of suds. I was aware that I was encroaching on her spot with a view of the barn and hayshed (perhaps with a deer nipping alfalfa from the stack). "I've been doing dishes for fifty years," she'd say. "I think I can manage these."

Only once did she tell me something about what washing dishes meant to her. She told me this in her last year, when dementia loosened parts of herself that held opinions she didn't share much, if at all. She told me quietly (as if telling a secret) that she never particularly *liked* doing the dishes, but it was a time she could reliably have all to herself. *No one would ever bother her while she did the dishes.* It was rare private time, with the advantage of not looking like private time at all. She could even invoke it with people still in the room. She smiled at this: "If something was going on at the table I didn't like, I just got up and started doing dishes."

I smiled, too. That description of doing dishes sounded less like drudgery and more like a personal magic trick, an escape that didn't even require leaving the room. It made dishes more than a job she did for the family. It was also a means to other ends that were all her own. The dishes were her thing, but that thing wasn't about the dishes at all.

170

It isn't metaphor to say *my heart aches.* I cry, but not at the moments cliché would expect. The family never had mourning practices except to avoid it publicly and wing it privately.

But rituals of mourning are a way to stay in, rather than flee, that place of mind and body the grieving would rather not be. And Dad soon develops his own ritual routine, each morning looking at pictures of their wedding and reading her obituary. He looks at her memorial book. A way to reconcile her ongoing presence with her obvious absence.

Then he pores over large paper maps of northern Wisconsin's Turtle Flambeau flowage. He peers at the spiky inlets through a magnifying glass or reads a page or two of its history. His eyes aren't what they used to be, but his memory is sharp. His imagination runs full force, and this exercise feeds it. Northern Wisconsin, the place of his birth and upbringing, represents his vitality. The ins and outs of the flowage, the characters associated with it, his memories of fishing it as a teen, the unlikely story of its coming to be. It's in his bones and will erupt in dreams.

171

Dad negotiates renewed grief over his mother. She died in April, too. As did Florence. April has a lot to answer for.

His mother died when he was three months old. Like Mom and Florence, she was a teacher, beautiful, lively, and popular. He recalls how strange it was as a boy, when people in town told him about her. *How could they know more about her than he ever would?*

His mother's sister and husband took him in. They'd just lost a baby boy. To these religious folks, it must've seemed like cruel and blessed providence. Meanwhile, his father worked a route as a traveling salesman for Standard Oil, remarrying a few years later and settling into a local job. He wanted to bring his son home, but the aunt and uncle refused to let him go. This boy was wanted by two families.

Dad was unaware of this tussle until he heard about it as an adult, but by then the heavy story of being abandoned by his father defined him. It would not budge. The fracture between them would never heal.

172

Ali invites us to plant a memorial tree in the West Hills garden behind the house. Dad helps Ali put dirt into the hole, and her teenage daughters pamper Dad with his favorite coffee in a paper cup with hand-drawn hearts. They give us photo gifts remembering Mom.

Back home, he puts the empty decorated coffee cup on top of the fridge, where he displays his birthday cards. We'll visit West Hills more over the summer, and every time he'll bring home another treasured cup. He'll collect a whole row along one edge of the fridge.

173

In the last weeks, her life seemed to boil down to two desires: to show love and to be loved. A stunning simplicity of being.

Nevertheless. Nevertheless. I think about all the years she spent bound up by insecurities. Only after all that was forgotten, after there was no more energy for the rehearsal of old traumas, did love prevail. Just expression and desire: friendship, chocolate, music, color, sleep.

A month later, after most of the paperwork and arrangements are done, I buckle under old, outdated family stories that heave up without warning. *What will it take for me to shed these anxieties, after years of work to unpick the knots? Will it take a physical decline? A bout with dementia? A failure of breath and slowing of blood? A confinement to bed? A daily humiliation over emptying my bowels? Is a physical humbling needed to settle the emotional clamor? What will it take for me to allow love to prevail, or is that a privilege reserved for the dying?*

174

I never learned how to say goodbye. We just left one place and landed somewhere else, running headlong into the next future. The imprint of military life, leavened with Depression-era stoicism and a dash of the Wallenda effect. Don't look down. Just go. And keep going.

175

So much grief. So little mourning. A mute scream settles in. A child's voice says, *I'm alone. I've been abandoned. I'm lost.*

Is this the story that vibrates as terror in bone? Is this molecular ache what some people can't name but throw back into the world, multiplying the pain?

From that disjointed place, injured and incoherent, how can anyone summon the grace to be kind to others? To be kind to ourselves?

176

Each stone marking the labyrinth path is a world populated by moss and lichen, with little Johnny-jump-up violets hugging them for warmth. I walk until I see something that stops me. I'll take a picture of whatever has caught my eye. Some detail of mottled gray continents fading to black, punctuated with dusty green frills or tiny flutes that catch rain and the occasional speck of orange, not so much clinging to the rock as cloaking it in slow life closer to the rock's own speed than these legs walking by.

I'll look at the picture tomorrow or the next day when my mind flees the scene and needs coaxing back. To remind me that beyond this world are many other worlds entirely unconcerned with what feels all-encompassing to me.

177

Dad's wavering balance is manageable in summer when walking on clear ground. But winter is around the corner. Should I move into the ranch house, so he's not alone? Is that what's required now? I don't want to think about it, and he doesn't want to talk about it. We leave it alone.

178

Thunder clouds roll through before dawn. The dark of rural night is obliterated by lightning diffused through miles of storm moving west to east, from the taller, younger Bitterroots to the older, rounded Sapphire range. The storm will dissipate during its slide across the valley. That's how weather works out here.

Before it ends, the siren calling volunteer firefighters from their beds will sound twice. From my bedroom window, I see thick strands of light jag for the ground. Spidery strands remind me of the permanent network of veins on my father's feet. Once, two strands connect with a loose mesh to make a ragged ladder, briefly lowered to earth.

Rain follows, just enough to refresh the air. Petrichor. A rooster calls dawn even before the eastern horizon turns pink.

Emerge

179

A summer, and then a fall on the sunroom's hard floor, next to the woodbox and plastic mat for outdoor boots. Dad was just up from his afternoon nap and letting the old border collie out the door. He's adamant: *It wasn't Lady's fault.*

Les and his dog Sammy usually leave for the day around 3:30 p.m., but Les tells me the Case tractor was on his mind. He and Dad had been mulling over a repair, and he had a new idea. Uncharacteristically, he went to the house to see if Dad was around for a talk over coffee. He knocked at the back door, and Dad yelled from the floor, "Come in!"

Les calls me, I grab my bag and go. Ten minutes later we're negotiating with Dad about calling an ambulance. *Nah,* he says, laying prone. He just wants an Advil. He's sure he can sleep it off. Can we get him to the couch? Maybe put a canvas under him and drag him there? I do as he says until the pain makes it clear to him that sleep isn't the cure for this problem.

180

In the local ER, an X-ray shows that the ball has snapped off the top of his femur. A nurse stitches up the meaty edge of one palm, split when he used it to break his fall. I hold his other hand while plans for a hip replacement surgery are made elsewhere. A hospital in Missoula has room in their schedule.

He's moved back to the gurney for another ambulance ride. I ask the paramedics if I should follow. *Nah,* they say. Visitors aren't allowed in the hospital. COVID rules. It'll be a wasted trip.

Decisions are accelerating. I have his health power of attorney paperwork, but Dad seems lucid, so they rely on his consent. I'm out of the picture unless I insist otherwise. It's a fight to be heard.

I clasp his hand again and tell him I'll be in touch with the hospital about what's happening. I'll figure out how I can be in touch with him. I'll tell the family.

What else does he need to hear?

A sudden thought settles on me: *He's 91, and no surgery is routine at that age. This may be the last time I ever see him.* But I don't say that. I can't let him see that.

He asks for some water. The paramedics push him to the door. He's still asking for water. They're talking over him.

Loudly, I ask, "Can he have a glass of water?" Not quite a scream, though that's there in the back of my throat. For a few seconds, the machine stops. He has a few sips, then closes his eyes. The gurney disappears down the hall.

I take a deep breath.

This won't do.

I know I can't follow him down the hall, so I run out the front entrance and around the side of the building to the ambulance bay. The ambulance doors stand open. The paramedics hang around the back, waiting for paperwork. I ask if I can see him, and they let me climb inside.

What did I say? What did he say? I don't remember. Whatever comes next, it will have to be enough.

181

I'm severed from his hospital stay by COVID protocols and medical efficiencies that don't have much time for the drag of families. My calls to the patient liaison roll to voicemail. Her call back goes to mine.

Finally, we connect. Surgery went well. He should be discharged in three days. He'll be using a standard walker. I can drop off things for him at the front desk, and they'll be taken to his room.

I write a letter with news of the ranch, print it out in a large-sized, readable font, put it in a bag with his glasses, hearing aids, the newspaper bridge column, and a slice of his favorite rhubarb pie, drive forty miles north, drop it at the front desk, turn around, and drive home.

I stand in the living room, the last time it'll be arranged as Mom and Dad lived in it. He won't be walking up and down the stairs at first, so the living room will have to be a temporary bedroom. It's a day's worth of rush to clear piles of books and move furniture to make room for a twin bed unearthed from a back bedroom. I source a bedside commode and recliner. Experience doing this for Mom comes in handy.

The width of the downstairs bathroom door, too narrow for a walker, is a problem. I call the neighbor who helped with our thought exercise when we considered Mom coming home. Can we widen the door? Structurally, he's not sure it's possible. We agree that Dad would hate any alteration. Let's think on it.

Dad won't want to sleep downstairs. I think again about whether I'd be able to help him up and down the stairs, remembering how he carried me, ten years old in a full body cast, up and down for a good six weeks. (That after three weeks strung up in hospital traction.

Treatment for a broken femur has changed since 1972.) Some part of me stubbornly believes that I should be able to return the favor, but the chance is high that we'd land at the bottom of the stairs in a busted heap.

Meanwhile, that twin bed becomes my own. While he's in the hospital, I stay at the ranch to take care of Lady and keep a presence at the house. Rather than sleep in my teenage bedroom (now Mom's sewing room), I like to be downstairs where I can hear Lady groaning and yipping in her sleep. Sometimes I get up in the dark to stroke her body, twitching in a dream before she sighs into a deeper place.

182

It takes a couple days to hit me: He fell around 3 p.m., and I wasn't due back at the ranch until the next morning at 10 a.m. Les' itch to discuss a tractor repair spared Dad hours of pain and very possibly his life.

What a stupid fulfillment of Dad's childhood abandonment story that would've been—lying on the floor, alone, colder and angrier by the hour, unable to move, unable to reach the phone, feeling the worst of his feelings about himself in the world come true. No way to live or die.

183

Every morning, I drop off a letter and snack. I'm told the news will be consumed, and the food will go in the trash. He's just not hungry.

I call the patient liaison. She says he won't be discharged after three days. Now she says it'll be a week. On the next call, the plan is for a couple weeks of intensive rehab, starting after the Labor Day weekend. The holiday comes and goes, and I get a call: No rehab. He's being discharged today to a nearby nursing home. His worst nightmare is in full swing.

What? Why? The liaison says he's been charming to the nurses, but he refuses pain medication other than Tylenol and doesn't want to do rehab. I get scraps, but it will take weeks to fully grasp that something in him has unraveled, something that will take much longer to heal than a hip replacement, if, indeed, it can ever heal at all.

I call Ali at West Hills. Dumb luck—she has room for him, and the hospital can discharge him to her care. The machine groans and grudgingly allows him to stay in the hospital one more night while Ali and I quickly outfit his room with the same hospital bed and furnishings Mom used. Later, we can make arrangements for visits from a home health nurse and physical therapist.

At first, he'll share a large room upstairs with another resident until, by chance, the single room downstairs that was Mom's becomes free. Private quarters befit an officer of upper rank, he tells me, and this familiar room where he and Mom shared their last moments together helps him feel close to her.

He knows Ali and trusts her. He knows the house and its other folks (not "inmates"). He'd rather be going home, but this is a world better than the anonymity of a nursing home miles away from the ranch. Did Mom prepare us for this, too?

184

His appetite is near zero. We try all his favorite foods from home as well as the fresh West Hills menu. Nothing appeals.

Bouts of constipation and incontinence alternate. Are his bowels shutting down?

He refuses the pain medication that would make rehab exercises bearable. He doesn't like to feel his mind go fuzzy.

He detests the walker. "I'm not gonna drag that thing around!" It offends his dignity in a way his handmade walking stick doesn't.

Why does he need rehab anyway? "I can walk just fine, if you'd just get out of my way!"

His mind is still frighteningly sharp. He recounts detailed stories from every period of his life. But his reasoning now leans toward some form of magical thinking. This is a new twist.

185

Weaker. Thinner. Nevertheless, he's settled on a plan to be home by spring. West Hills is a cozy place to spend the winter, and by the time April rolls around, calves will be on the ground and water will be running. He'll be home then, he says. I want to believe it.

He dreams vividly and in the morning reports that he walked all around the house. Given that evidence, why are we telling him that he needs us to help him get to the toilet? The facts he builds in his mind are now stronger than reality he can test with his body.

He's no longer quite here in the mundane world of cause and effect. Where there's no way forward or backward, he goes sideways. That disconnect preserves his belief in his own strength and capability, despite the physical evidence. Is it hallucination feeding delusion? Maybe. But naming it doesn't change anything.

186

What does he mean when he says he wants to go back to the ranch? Does he mean that he wants to go back to the patch of ground where he's lived for the last 50 years? Or does he also mean that he wants to return to life in his prime, his body obeying his mind and Mom at his side?

If turning back the clock is his real aim, being able to walk again isn't the problem or solution. I recall what he told Mom once when she pleaded for him to take her home to the house where she was a teenager: "Honey, that place exists only in your imagination."

187

After some weeks, he fires the home health nurse outright and (more politely) ends the physical therapist visits (though he wouldn't mind seeing that PT who talks with him about hunting pheasants). He's had it with their cajoling, nudges, and stern urging.

He's heard all their warnings about becoming permanently bed-bound and the pain of pressure sores. This is his future if he doesn't gain some strength back. He's heard all the consequences, and it's not enough to break the spell that's been unleashed on him. He dismisses them all: "If you wanna preach, I can point you to a church down the street!"

188

Months ago, reaching through his grief for a grip on each day, he told me his recipe for happiness:

Someone to love
Something to do
Something to look forward to

At that time, he'd lost the first of those. Now, it seems that he's lost all three.

189

What does he need? What are we missing? Ali and I talk long about what's going on with Dad. We work with a chronic care nurse through Dad's doctor to manage the all-important bowel routine. The nurse is available for advice and prescriptions, but the real care is in Ali's hands.

Her care isn't transactional. She's that professional caregiver everyone wants for their loved one, a mind and heart that seek to understand. This is the slow medicine that comes down to patient, hands-on care and close observation. I bring a knowledge of his history, and that helps her assess how to proceed.

She tells me that eldercare is a vocation. She wasn't able to be with her own father in his last years. She's honored to care for mine.

190

"Too many women around!" he complains one day. I arrange for Les to visit. I serve them coffee in the familiar cups from home then wait on the porch while they talk. It's hard for Les to see him this way, but the visit does Dad a world of good.

191

Dad wakes and tells Ali that he's shot a bear. He wants her to go with him down the hill, where the bear carcass is, to skin and gut it. In this scenario, he's about eighteen years old. He says that while he was walking back to town he saw the light on at West Hills. He remembered that he could push the call button for Ali's help—and here she is!

She tells him it was a dream, but he insists it all happened. And it did, so powerfully in his mind that it has lodged in his body. By afternoon, he's told the story several times, each time with more or different details. Each time someone suggests it was a dream, his heels dig in deeper.

He tells me that the bear carcass rolled on top of him, covering him in urine and feces. That's why he was walking back to town, to get cleaned up. I wonder if his flesh, feeling his incontinence, provoked that image? The weight he felt on his chest... did he have a small heart attack in the night? Have real physical details been transposed into dream language? If we can decode the dream, will we get a new clue about his condition?

Is this partly a memory? The setting is northern Wisconsin, but Uncle Bill tells me there were no bears there in their youth. Dad has never hunted bear, but he respects their legendary strength. To kill one says something about human survival against forces much greater than ourselves.

He finally concedes, "Maybe that bear's still down there, or maybe it's already been skinned and the meat packed up. I don't care. I don't really like bear meat."

He tells the story with a seamless transition from his young, mobile self slaying the bear to his current self at West Hills where Ali cares for him. I wonder aloud whether he's experiencing time in a different way? Maybe, somehow, right now his 18-year-old self is as near to him as his 91-year-old self?

He doesn't like that. "Are you saying I'm *losing* it?"

"No, I'm not saying you're losing it. I think that—maybe—you're just experiencing time differently right now." He relaxes and doesn't disagree.

192

Why is his body shutting down while his mind marches on? The prosaic explanation some visitors put forward (with a grave sigh): *He's dying of a broken heart.*

But what's happening doesn't feel that straightforward. This isn't a romance novel. A simple story of marital devotion and loss will be complicated in coming months.

He will die of a broken *body*, betrayed by the guts and muscles and appetites that have almost always done his bidding. Meanwhile, *he wants more life.* He wants to be eighteen again. He wants another run at it. He'll show us that he loves falling in love and being in love more than loving any one person.

This doesn't mean he loves Adele any less. She was for many years his reason for *doing.* But he's making it clear that she was never his reason for *being.*

193

I call the surgical center to cancel his six-week check-in. He hasn't made any progress, and I worry that two hours in the car and multiple wheelchair transfers will be too painful and exhausting.

I describe his ongoing issues to the nurse, and I hear concern and resignation in her voice. She knows what's coming, though I'm still optimistically wondering how we reverse the tide so he can eventually come home.

She sighs, "Oh, honey. Good luck."

He doesn't want to ever go back to a hospital. No more ambulance rides for any reason. Ali can honor his wishes if he has a POLST (Provider's Orders for Life-Sustaining Treatment) in place.

I'm glad that he's asked for this, in so many words. The dreaded swarming of ambulance and coroner (or, in the coroner's absence, sheriff or deputy) is acutely in my mind. I know he wouldn't want to be attended in death by what he'd angrily call a "circus."

Dad's doc generously makes the short trek from his clinic to West Hills to fill out the POLST. Dad notices that he's wearing a canvas jacket. Not a white coat in sight. This feels like a social visit. They chat for about an hour, the doctor sitting bedside, jotting notes, hearing about the encounter with the bear. They talk about other things men talk about in this landscape—weather, water, cattle, vehicles. Dad enjoys the visit and invites him to stop by again.

Outside on the porch, I ask the doc what he thinks. When will Dad be able to go home? In the spring? Or sooner? What's realistic?

He takes one breath then delivers his unadorned conclusion: Dad has a zero percent chance of going home. He's suffering from a failure to thrive. (That's no longer a diagnosis, but it still communicates the gist of the matter.) I've only ever heard it used to explain why a newborn, for no apparent reason, dies. It's a term that gives up on "why."

In an earlier day, Dad would've described the situation this way: "The surgery was a success, but the patient died." The doctor says we can activate hospice anytime.

195

The ground tilts. And my nose won't stop dripping. Am I getting sick? Or is it just the tears? Do I have COVID? I take my temperature. Normal.

Am I forgetting to breathe? I remind myself to breathe.

I go into this day after a night awake, staring at the ceiling, weighing what came before and what may come next. The weight of what's ahead—activating hospice, with the cover story that it can be ended when Dad improves, knowing that he likely will not, and that this is another threshold toward his last.

The slow roll of Mom's decline brought the mixed blessing of time to get used to the eventuality. This, despite Dad being 91, feels sudden. Is that my own denial talking? The disorder in my body echoes what jangles beyond thought.

<h1 align="center">196</h1>

Dad is peeved. He knows well what hospice means. He looks from me to Ali and back: "Are you giving up on me?"

Ali is emphatic: We're *not* giving up on him. We're here to help him in every way we can. We still believe he can turn this around. If his appetite improves and he stops losing muscle. If he can swap the magical thinking for the practical work of rebuilding his strength. If we can get his gut back on track. The priority now isn't measuring improvement. It's managing chronic conditions like appetite, bowel routines, and skin health, to give him time for whatever he needs more time for. And all that will be easier if we have access to care that's in line with his condition and wishes right now.

And the parts I don't say to him: Hospice will help us manage the increasingly frequent dreams and visual hallucinations that blend into delusion. And, if our optimism fails, hospice will help him do whatever work is left, likely of a more ephemeral sort.

I remind him that Mom graduated from hospice. She showed us that it's possible. He's still peeved.

We remind him that if he's on hospice, the home health nurse and physical therapists will definitely not be back. He relaxes. Well then, that's okay.

197

We meet with a hospice planner. Dad's eyes are sunken in a way I haven't seen before. He's charming to her, especially after he notices that she's left-handed, as he and I are.

"I'm sorry it took breaking my leg to meet you," he says. He agrees to hospice, "if that means you'll come back to visit."

A world away from the volatile mood he was in yesterday. I was prepared for rudeness and refusal, but today he's sharp and reasonable. He tells her stories about Wisconsin, and because she's from the same town as a cousin, he tells her about that cousin's fiery death a few years ago. She and her car were found charred on a railroad track near her home. By the car's position it seemed she was driving on the track as if it was a road. The car's undercarriage on the rails must've made sparks that…

Why was she on the tracks? No one knows. He never says, "What a grisly way to go" or "I miss my cousin." He shakes his head and tells the story.

198

It's 7 p.m., and I'm already in bed. Dark evenings head toward the longest nights of winter. Really, too early to go to sleep but with no brain to focus. No interest in anything. Much as Dad describes his state. Where do you put your mind when you have no attention to pay?

199

He says he's getting out of bed to go to the bathroom. He throws the covers back and shuffles his legs to the edge of the bed. Ali and I slow him down.

He refuses to use the walker and wheelchair. *Of course he can walk to the bathroom! Last night he walked down the hill and back again!* He points out the glass doors to the far side of the valley and reports that he's been watching ranchers on horseback driving cows and calves across the river. They could use his help.

Evidence that his legs no longer bear his weight has no place in this other mind he's developed, where he is young, vital, strong, capable, and needed. The uselessness of the sick bed offends everything he believes about himself.

When he's alone, he'll try again to get out of bed and will collapse down the side. Ali will find him lying on the floor, patiently waiting for help. As he did after the fall that broke his hip, lying on the sunroom floor uncomplaining, then asking to be put on the couch, where he was sure he could sleep it off.

200

He wakes in the afternoon from a dream that he's going home for Thanksgiving. "Get me dressed!" We do and get him in the wheelchair. Then exhaustion hits.

Would I like to split a beer with him? We do, an echo of his 4 p.m. routine of some years. He carefully tilts his glass and pours beer down the side to minimize the foam. He takes a sip and screws up his face—says it tastes *triple* carbonated.

In the last few days he's complained that his usual vegetable juice tastes so salty that it dries out his mouth. Hospice tells me that dehydration and electrolyte imbalance are making him extra sensitive to certain tastes and textures.

I bring him low-sodium vegetable juice. That, at least, is an easy fix.

201

After sitting up in the wheelchair for a half hour or so, he's had enough. It takes a couple of tries for him to stand up at the walker and pivot into bed. Nevertheless, he says he wants to go back to the ranch and stay overnight—"at least."

He wants to die in his own bed. If I take him home for a night and manage to get him up the stairs to his bedroom, maybe that's what will happen. Maybe he's thinking of the gun that he kept by the bed. I don't know where it is, but maybe he does.

I want to give him what he wants, but I also want him to have reliable, safe care. Even if he comes home for a day, it won't be a return to the routine he remembers, up and down the stairs, down to the barn with a turn by his machine shop.

And I can't care for him the way Ali does. He won't let me help with the toilet or clean-up from incontinence. The modesty between parent and child is intact (and the day it goes missing will be another mark of decline).

He's so capable of traveling in his mind. What's the tradeoff between the physical place and his ability to project himself there? Is one a reasonable substitute for the other? When Mom wanted to "go home," she was asking for the impossible, home being a brick house in her mind. But when Dad asks to go home, it's a real place within reach. How can we give him what he wants and also keep him safe without making him feel, as he puts it, like a prisoner?

202

Ali finds Dad, once again, lying quietly on the floor, this time with his head under the bed. He comments on the mechanics of the hospital bed's undercarriage.

Later, he's unusually quiet. I ask how he is. "I'm still here."

He thinks Ali is mad at him for getting on the floor. I tell him she's not mad, but I'm sure she was scared for him, as am I.

He half-recalls a T.S. Eliot line: "How does the world end? Not with a bang but a whimper." He says that when Ali was helping him up, he saw a tall figure standing behind her. "The Grim Reaper?" he wonders. Later, he'll consider whether it was one of the tall hospice nurses before dismissing it as a shadow.

He says to Ali, "I guess you're not letting me go."

"Go where?"

"To where Adele went."

He has a coherent, thoughtful phone call with his younger sibling Bill. Not the usual reserve of older brother in control. He says he's had a good scare and ends the call with "I love you," an uncharacteristic offer of tenderness.

203

Why does he keep trying to get out of bed? Is he falling back on the habit of decades, getting up half-asleep to go downstairs and make a fire in the wood stove?

204

On a day of many bowel movements, he insists on walking to the toilet. I bring the wheelchair over.

No, he says, he's getting out of bed and walking to the toilet.

I bring the walker to his bedside.

No, he's getting out of bed and *walking* to the toilet.

I remind him he hasn't walked in over three months. He doesn't believe me, so I count off on my fingers: September, October, November.

I call Ali, and she comes just in time to talk him back into bed. But now he's suspicious that we're manipulating him. He says we're lying to him about his capabilities—"brainwashing" him to be less confident about what he can do.

This is a new problem. Delusion is slipping into paranoia. If he doesn't trust us, this situation could become hellish for everyone. If he wants to be pissed off at me, that's one thing. I see him a few hours each day. But Ali's here for every minute of the day and night, and he must trust her now as much as he trusted her when she cared for Mom.

205

He's settling accounts. He says a few weeks ago he walked out of Ford's, the small local department store founded the same year he was born, with a pair of red sneakers. He tells me to go there and pay for the shoes. I say I will, but could I see the sneakers, so I know how to describe them to the clerk?

Sure, he says. They're stashed around here somewhere. Maybe in his other room? He believes he sleeps in a different bed every night and has multiple rooms in the house, though all are decorated with pictures of him and Mom, which strikes him as odd.

206

Dad's bored. He wants to go for a drive. The day is sunny, the winter roads clear. We've taken drives to the ranch, across the cattle guard and around past the garage, root cellar, apple trees, stock trailer, machine shop, and machine shed to pull up at the crescent of barn, corral, and hay shed. I call Les, so we can cross paths for a few minutes. Soon, Dad's energy flags, and he waves me on to finish the loop past the red woodshed, the pasture that leads to the pond, the bull pasture where Les' young ones are growing, the house, and back onto the road.

Ali and I make these field trips seem ordinary and relaxed. They're nerve-racking for me, but I don't tell him that. I'm more aware of his fragility than he is. I'm braced for mood swings that can pitch up out of nowhere.

Ali gets him up and dressed. He thinks we're humoring him and won't actually get him into the car, but all the transfers work. He has everything he needs: jacket, red plaid wool hat, sunglasses, Wint-O-Green Life Savers, tissues, gloves. In the car, he puts his hands together in prayer (a comment on my driving). His grin says he's joking.

Today, he wants to see something new, so I drive south on a back-road that runs along the base of the mountains, slowly, so he can take in the scenery, scrubby fields with pine trees, empty of houses, cows here and there. After a few miles, we turn east, then pick up the highway that runs north back through town. At the intersection we might turn right to the old Eastside highway or turn left back to West Hills.

It's enough. Go left. "A good effort," he says.

207

Dad dreams that he's in a church, lying down. This seems strange to him, so he gets up and goes outside to plant a garden.

In the morning, he tells me he planted a garden in a patch northeast of his room. A few days later, he wonders if we should go out and check on it. Maybe some seeds have come up?

I ask what he planted: carrots, lettuce, radishes, cucumbers, green onions. The garden of his boyhood on his aunt and uncle's farm. The garden of my girlhood on his farm. It's January, the frozen month when seed catalogs usually come in the mail and planning for spring begins.

208

Dad has twice described hearing people outside his room singing music so lovely he barely has words for it. The first time, it's two gray-haired ladies sitting at the dining table. He wants to give them lingonberry jam for singing so beautifully.

Another time he says the singing comes from people in a car parked in the driveway. He says they played music that so transported him that he wanted to go out there and ask them what it was. Are these angels, he tentatively suggests, coming to sing to him about the next place?

209

Florence, the last alive of her eight brothers and sisters, had a series of nighttime events in the weeks before she died. At 3:30 a.m., she woke from sleep in her recliner concerned about somewhere she had to go and whether she was ready. "What will I wear? I'm not even dressed."

She wanted her feet on the ground. *On the ground.*

She said she had to fit in a box, and it was very small. The box was "129." She would be the last one through, and when she was through she had to say, "129." It was very important to say that. She asked to write it down, so she'd remember. I gave her a marker and small pad of paper. She shakily wrote the number. I tore the paper from the pad, crumpled it into a ball and tucked it in her hand. She gripped it tightly.

"I don't know... I don't know... I don't know..." She was somewhere else but looking at me for help. I remembered hospice's advice for these moments and suggested that she did know, deep inside. Maybe there was someone she could ask? Her mother? Her dad?

She bent forward, arms reaching down, her chest on her knees. She said she had to get small—small enough to get in the box—129 was *very* small.

She asked me what she had to do to get small enough. I said I wasn't sure. Maybe there was something that had to be left behind? Or maybe the box was bigger than she thought? Or maybe there was someone to ask? Whatever the answer, she could find it.

She struggled to get small but apparently not small enough. "I don't know... I don't know..."

She wore herself out with the effort. Did she want to rest? Maybe the answer would come in her sleep? She thought about that and agreed, though with a tinge of defeat.

She said in a small voice, "I have to get big again…" and sat up. Then pushed her shoulders back and said in her loudest voice, "I HAVE TO GET BIG AGAIN!" She leaned back into the chair, and said quietly, sadly, "I have to get big again."

She slept and woke a few hours later wanting to take a walk. With her walker, she went slowly across the room, pivoted, and returned to her chair. She smiled as she plopped back in the recliner. "I feel good!" she said, with a satisfied, signature nod.

She dozed and when she woke an hour later didn't remember anything about 129 or getting small or the box. She also didn't remember taking that short walk but wasn't surprised that she had.

210

He asks again if he can hitch a ride home to get his red truck. He wants to have it nearby, in case he wants to buy a sportsman's license. He wants to be ready when fishing season opens.

The truck has a topper outfitted for fly fishing. He'd bought it just after he sold the herd. He was finally going to have time for fishing. Too soon, the tremor's effect on his balance made wading into rivers and streams unwise.

I ask if it would be enough if I drive it here and park it where he can look at it while we visit. "But then how will *you* get home?" he reasons.

He's joked for years that we could bury him in that truck, like a Viking laid in a ship, set on fire, and pushed out to sea. The image has a strange resonance in the wake of him recalling his cousin's fiery death in her car.

Ali and I talk about it. The truck is taller than my car, and boosting him up into the passenger seat wouldn't be easy. But it might be possible.

The following day, I bring the red truck to take him for a drive. He doesn't recognize it.

211

This post-surgical decline, I learn, is a thing that sometimes happens to elderly people who undergo general anesthesia. Research is sparse. Notions about the condition are vague. The theory is that general anesthesia sets off inflammation (maybe), which sets off neurological and metabolic changes (sometimes).

Signs of dementia are typical. But this isn't like Mom's dementia, a general deterioration that followed the patterns of Alzheimer's disease. In Dad, it feels like something broke. As if some part of him experienced anesthesia as death, and the rest of him is now slowly catching up to the part that's already moved on.

212

Worry spirals. Uncertainty is a constant, but there's no putting off daily care decisions to meet his evolving needs. We make informed guesses with best intentions, aware of how devastatingly wrong those can go.

I also hear the echo of something Dad has repeated over the years: *Doubt can get you killed.* He learned it as a career Cold War military officer. A suboptimal decision is better than no decision at all.

Michelle puts it another way: As a caregiver I act with best intentions, but there are often times I just can't know if I've done the right thing. That's the reality. And second guessing or beating myself up afterward won't serve me or the next hour's care that I must be ready to give. A deeply kind and practical piece of advice.

213

Is Dad rallying? His appetite's a bit better, and he declares that he'll be home for his birthday in late January. He tells the hospice nurse he just needs to gain a pound of muscle a day, and he'll soon be strong enough to walk.

This practical man is no longer in the realm of the practical. He's never been afraid of hard work or pushing through pain. This isn't refusal to do the work. It's a delusion that the work is irrelevant. He believes he'll wake up one day and be back to his strong self. Reality will bend to his will. His certainty is both heartbreaking and strangely convincing.

My own magical thinking creeps in. I still occasionally wonder if he could make it happen. His will is so strong. Is incontinence reversible? Would eating more reverse the muscle wasting and mood swings? Can the long hours of sleep that signal degeneration become regenerative?

I privately toy with the pipe dream, while fearing what he'd experience by hanging on. Being bedbound is not a life he wants. He's tolerating it now on the back of the sheer belief that it's all a bad dream. He'll wake up soon. That delusion takes energy.

How long can he keep it up?

He must, in his own quiet moments, know the score. He must in some way recognize the gaps between what he wants and what is physically possible. I think this but saying it out loud would be a betrayal.

214

He's agreed to take medication to help with the blur between dreams and waking life. It helps him sleep more soundly. More important, he's less paranoid, back in a trusting frame of mind.

Ali and I have become more nimble in accommodating his reality. I remember Mom seeing angels and being reminded that my reality is only part of the picture here. Dad's perception, as much as possible, leads. If it's safe to follow and it makes him happy, why not?

He wakes from an afternoon nap and tells Ali he just went fishing. He's brought back enough trout to feed the house, but they need to be cleaned. Ali should call me to clean the fish, then she can cook them up for supper. They're in a cooler right outside the door.

The next day, I buy a big steelhead filet at the grocery store, as close to trout as they have. Ali cooks it up with cornmeal crust, the way Dad likes it. He eats a little, and some other folks in the house have some.

"Did everyone get enough?" he wants to know. "Did everyone get fed?"

Yes. Yes.

215

He picks little fights. Contradicts me over nothing. I don't think he believes what he's saying. What matters is the opposition. He asserts his will to test my response.

Am I still listening to him? Does his opinion count? Am I taking his wishes seriously? Is he still in charge?

216

This week has been a long month.

217

COVID-19 deaths pass the half-million mark in the U.S. So many souls on the wing.

218

Dad's working through a bucket list. One item: He wants to go to the McDonald's drive-thru and get a Big Mac. Over the years, he's seen TV commercials for it but never had one.

I suspect his patience will run out before we're able to move through the typically long line. How about I go and get him a burger? If he really likes it, we can do the whole thing next time.

By the time I return with the burger, he's asleep. A few days later, Ali gets him a fresh one. His assessment: "We don't need to do that again."

219

Another bucket list item: He wants a snowblower. He's never had one, having skipped from hand shovel to tractor for snow removal. Les has one, and he's seen how handy it is for making walking paths and clearing tight spaces. He wants one of his own. He has the money, there's a dealer in town with good pricing, and he won't be deterred.

He first wants to discuss it with Les, so we go to the ranch. This is usually the limit of his strength, but when I suggest we go to the ranch supply store the following day he waves me on, determined.

At the store, I park near the row of shiny red machines, and a clerk wheels one around to the open passenger door. Dad looks at it from his seat, leans out a little to touch it, asks a few questions. He tells the clerk he looks forward to using it, though he won't be the one who'll use it the most. He nods and waves me inside to buy it.

When I come out of the store, I can't see him in the car. *Fuckety fuck fuck fuck. Did he get out of the car? Did he fall on the asphalt?* When I get closer, I see he's slumped forward in the seatbelt, so exhausted he needed a rest from holding himself up.

Back at West Hills, I wait for him to proudly tell Ali that he bought a snowblower! But he's not proud. He's angry and impatient. "When's it gonna be delivered?" "When's it gonna snow enough to test it out?" *"How do we even know it works?"*

What's eating him? Why can't he enjoy his monumental effort? A nurse will declare that this is the first time anyone ever got up from their hospice bed to buy a snowblower.

I'm reminded of the last item in his recipe for happiness: something to look forward to. He's worked mightily to find that over the last months. And now that the snowblower is his, that very short list is one item shorter.

At 4 a.m., a lifelong usual wake-up time, Dad calls Ali to turn on his light and find his glasses. He wants to read the user manual.

When I see him a few hours later, he looks so tired, voice low. Our outing reminds me how hard he pushed himself last summer mowing hay, a sort of defiance that, if it could speak, might say, "I'm gonna get this done, and if *this* is what kills me, so be it."

Winter has always been his planning time, sitting at the kitchen table with a cup of coffee and graph paper or yellow legal pad, making notes and sketches. Purpose in the works. Does Dad now know (in the as-yet-unspoken part of him) that there's a good chance his winter plans will not see the spring? That the time for repair has passed, and even the maintenance done during winter months in preparation for the busy growing season is now moot?

221

A lone red-and-black carpenter ant moves, slow leg by slow leg, across icy terrain of the labyrinth path. Where did it come from? Where is it going? It's 42 degrees today, balmy for winter, but still inhospitable.

I watch its slow-motion progress in the direction of more snow and ice, think about it, then put my gloved finger near. It clings to the tip. I take it to a lavender bush poking through the snow and set it down on a stalk with a sheltered path to clear earth.

Did I help? Or hurt? Does my small intervention matter? I nudged an ant's trajectory, possibly changing everything. Or nothing. I can't know, but I still have to act in good faith, with kindness in mind.

222

Dad wants to look his best for a sibling's visit. He asks me if his hair is okay. I comb it and wet down the wild bits. We've trimmed his unruly eyebrows, beard, and overgrown mustache. He has a fresh flannel shirt on and, under the covers, no pants. He's most comfortable this way, and those who don't need to know won't.

He wants his glasses in the breast pocket of his shirt. His wallet is in his bedside drawer. His pocketknife and tissues are on the tray. This arrangement will work but isn't ideal. He sums up the basic problem: "There aren't enough pockets in a shirt to make up for a lack of pants."

223

Dad describes how the sun came up this morning, first hitting the poinsettia on the windowsill and lighting up the red leaves. They fairly glowed. Then the sun reached the picture of him and Mom standing in front of his tractor fitted with a grapple.

He had really wanted a photo of just the grapple, but I put him and Mom in the frame. He's a little disappointed that the grapple is obscured, but he likes how he and Mom look.

"There's so much to enjoy," he says.

224

Once again, Ali finds Dad on the floor by the side of the bed. He says ranchers came to his room and asked him to help them load up a Charolais bull he'd been watching out his window. Maybe they're taking it to the livestock sale? They asked for his help, and he didn't want to be rude.

225

Today he's determined to *get outta here*. He tells me to pack up some of his things—boots, Stetson hat, coat, and a few other odds and ends. We're taking them home. If he can't be there, at least his stuff will be. At home. Where he and his stuff belong.

He makes the heroic effort to dress and help Ali with the transfers from bed to wheelchair to car. We park at the ranch, and he watches me take his things into the house. I put them on the couch, waving and pointing through the living room window. That's where he wants them.

Now he wants me to pull up to the garage, so he can get out of the car and take a leak by the root cellar. I shake my head. He negotiates: "I won't get out of the car. I'll just swing one leg out." He wants to mark his territory. He wants me to know that this is still his place, and I better not forget it.

226

The labyrinth follows the design set into Chartres Cathedral's floor stones in the early 13th century. At the heart of it are six areas that surround the center stone. These stations, shaped like petals or lobes, mark a continuum of six forms: mineral, plant, animal, human, angelic, and divine.

It's usual to walk clockwise around the center stone, moving from mineral around the circle to divine, what many would consider an ascent in form and complexity. I find myself walking the other way, coming down to earth, away from the realms of mystery to ground myself in mineral—clearly now the stuff of my mother, soon the stuff of my father, and one day the stuff that remains of a being that was called by my name.

227

When we moved to the ranch, the post and barbed-wire fences were falling down. They were supposed to keep cattle in but often let them out. As a new rancher, Dad decided to refurbish those boundaries with deep-planted posts chemically treated to prevent rot. In rocky soil, that's doing it the hard way, but he was told it was the way to build a fence that would last a lifetime. "Build for the ages," he would say of any construction project.

He was offended when, a mere forty years later, some fenceposts started to lean. Forty years was not, in his book, a lifetime. Nevertheless, underground the bottoms were rotting. He was outliving his fence.

Digging post holes takes a younger man's strength, so he took to planting steel fence posts alongside the leaning wooden ones and wiring them all together for stability. That shortcut was unthinkable in earlier days, but now it was a reasonable adaptation. We do what we can with the strength we have.

"We live too damned long," he says to me now. I wonder what adaptations he's cooking up while he looks out his windows for signs of wildlife. He seems to be willing himself to the end in a state of mind that all is still possible, as his dreams tell him even while his body disagrees. When I ask him if I can get him anything, he says, "Yeah! Another twenty good years!"

228

"It's good to see you," I say in the morning.

"It's good to be here to be seen," he answers.

229

Dad turns 92. I give him red Converse High Tops, the subject of his dream-delusion a few months back. A couple weeks ago, he said he really wanted to go shopping at Ford's for those red sneakers.

Uh oh. Is the delusion back? I'd been to Ford's and could report that they didn't sell red sneakers.

"That doesn't matter. Can we get them online?"

Ah! He's asking for a this-world wish.

I pulled up pictures of red sneakers on my phone until he lit up at the Converse High Tops, the sneakers he had as a kid. He wore them to wade in creeks, exploring and fishing. He wanted a new pair (in his favorite color red), so he could be ready when spring comes, though he admits that wading in a creek will be difficult because of his balance.

Today, in bed, he tries on this real pair and smiles at his feet poking out from under the covers. He'll wear them to his birthday party with the rest of the house in a few hours. There, he'll beg Nurse Ed to break him out, wheel him out the front door and down the snowy driveway in a movie-style escape. Maybe he's remembering one of his favorite films, *Butch Cassidy and the Sundance Kid.* He admires the idea of a life lived on its own terms (forgetting that those lives are never as heroic or buoyant as the stories we tell about them). Sure, it ends in a standoff and shootout, but they meet that death with humor and aplomb, heroes of their own story.

230

He wants to know the time. "About 12:30," I say.

"I didn't ask *about* what time! I asked the time!"

"12:29 and 13 seconds."

"Thank you." He sinks back into his pillow.

The precision is a holdover from his days as an Air Force navigator before digital computers, when tracking exact time was critical to charting a course. Across oceans of space and time, he always got his crew where they needed to be when they expected to get there.

On the ranch, he started every early morning with a fix on Greenwich Mean Time from a shortwave radio, adjusting his watch and the living room clock. Even before the world was synched through digital devices, our household was always on time.

Now he wants a clock on the wall, but it's too far away for him to see it. I get a digital clock with large glowing numbers, but he tears at the cord. I suspect the red numbers in the night are more disturbing than useful.

231

Aunt Florence's thing was sheets. From her bed, weeks from the end, she would point at her closet and ask if there were enough clean sheets. "Enough for what?" I asked.

Some 85 years earlier, she and her father had stood in the driveway of the family home in northern Wisconsin, watching a car make its way up their road. The cousins from Pennsylvania were arriving with no warning. A letter must've gone missing in the mail. Her father's first question to her: "Do we have enough clean sheets?"

She couldn't forget this. Being unprepared was a sort of terror in that world of rare long journeys and laundry that took a day or more to do. Her mother dead and older sisters out of the house, she was a teenager and also woman of the house. Was she good enough at it? Was she taking care of her father as well as those absent women would?

"Are there enough clean sheets?" she asks me.

"Yes, you have plenty," I tell her and think, *yes, you're prepared. Whoever or whatever comes, you have what you need. You're ready.*

She slept, and I wondered what my version of "enough clean sheets" would be. Maybe something about a safe parking place for my car. Across seven cities, I almost never had off-street parking, and parking on the street can be hard to trust. Will I miss a parking ban for street cleaning or snow emergency? Wake up to a ticket on the windshield or (much worse) a blank spot at the curb because my car was towed? Yeah, my worry will be about parking.

232

Florence. Mom. Dad. I feel, again, for the third time, the rhythms of hospice. The regularity of the clock and surges of activity, slow U-turns and accelerating arcs, flow, and ebb…

By attending to them, I also attend to myself. It's impossible not to. We're entangled. I carry that sense in mind, body, twitching eye, and gurgling gut.

Am I hospicing parts of myself, the ones that no longer serve me and are ready to die? Is that what I'm also doing here, underneath it all?

233

Dying will not be optimized. Not if the goal is dignity, comfort, and grace. The process defies calculation. We begin with routine, but it nearly always breaks when a different need erupts.

Ali and I follow Dad's stray thoughts into the place he inhabits today. We don't want to miss the opportunity that lurks in what strays. I know where his body is going. Materiality is evident. But so much else is happening invisibly. What arrogance it would be to sweep that away prematurely, just because my eyes can't register what moves in him now.

I think about this in the spring as I rake the woodchip path of the labyrinth. I will think about this in the fall when, bent over or on my knees, I trim the lavender plants. I work steadily but stop to take in the Steller's jays, sometimes scolding with a hawk-like scream or sitting in a nearby tree cackling or warbling. So many voices.

This all takes the time it takes. There are shortcuts, but why?

234

Dad says he needs to get to his new job harvesting potatoes, in a town to the north across the river. The crew may not be big enough to get the job done. He's worried he won't be able to get all the potatoes in before the frost.

I tell him I wouldn't worry about it.

He chastises me: "I know *you* won't worry about it, but *I* will."

235

Dad has been on hospice for three months, so he needs to be recertified for continued care. The recertification isn't in question. He's still losing weight and muscle mass. He sleeps about twenty hours a day. He's more often confused. His appetite is better than just after the surgery, but at most he takes in 500 calories a day, lately much of that chocolate. Mercifully, bowel movements are more regular.

I already know how he'd prefer to go—suddenly, "with my boots on." After Mom died, he told me a story about how a friend went. Early morning, this man goes to the woods to meet his hunting party. He arrives early at the meeting point. He sits down to wait, leans against a tree, cradling his rifle. He's found there by his friends, dead of a heart attack.

Not a bad way to go, Dad said, on your way to doing something you love. And he knows that such an end is no longer possible for him. He won't die with his boots on. That is not his path.

236

I never wanted my father's life, but here I am occupying its outlines, living in his house to take care of Lady. She's seventeen years old now but still spry enough to patrol around the house and barn. She's on the move until she flops down with a sigh on her bed or concrete step by the front door, paws dangling over the edge.

I wake, as he would, before sunrise to build a fire in the wood stove, let Lady out, fetch the newspaper, and take water to the barn cat on frozen mornings. I no longer disappear for hours into a book. The fire will go out, and the house will sink into cold.

I remain vigilant. His routine occupies me.

237

I was never much of a ranch kid. I wanted to be in a city. Like my mother, I wanted sidewalks and museums and concert halls and people who didn't look or sound like me. I like the anonymity typical in cities, not needing to know everyone's history three generations deep but still able to exchange a smile or simply share the same air.

I don't want to know other people's business, but in this valley knowing and being known is a sort of currency. Mom and Dad are respected here, and I can't deny that being their daughter lends me instant credibility. I'm earning the rest through presence and action, being here and doing, day in and day out.

Anonymity (wanting it or having it) is suspect here. I still want it. I still need space for the parts of me that don't fit this valley.

238

Three years ago now, driving through northern Utah to Montana, I pulled off the highway at a small roadside truck stop. A man smiled, wistful, and held the door open for me. Of ambiguous age. Thirties? Forties? Fifties? Round head with a wispy combover of golden-red strands, a natural color or maybe dyed and fading? Wearing a lived-in track suit. Fingernails chewed short and half-covered with a pale pink manicure, chipped but still hanging on. Did he also have a shadow of pink lipstick?

I smiled back. *Is he sad or do I imagine that?* After I peed and picked out more liquids for the rest of the drive, I stood in line behind him at the counter. The older woman at the register seemed like someone named Dottie or Marge. Silver bouffant flip hairdo, teased up to balance thick black mascara and aggressive blush. She asked him how he was doing, with what sounded like genuine tenderness. They talked a little, not worrying that I was waiting.

I didn't mind. I felt a shot of relief imagining that he has people who are kind to him in this place where men with pink nail polish are beyond out of place.

239

This is the first morning that Dad doesn't know who I am. He's on a train traveling across northern Wisconsin. We're at a whistle-stop, and I'm the steward bringing him breakfast.

I give him his usual newspaper bridge column, folded to size. He takes it eagerly. "This must be the schedule."

He asks me where I sleep (as a worker on the train). He asks me other questions to make small talk with someone he expects will be serving him for the duration of the trip. When I get ready to leave, he asks if I'll bring him supper later. Ali assures him that she'll bring him something to eat. "Do you work for the railroad, too?"

He points to his coffee cup: "Do I have time for a refill before we get going again?"

"You have time."

Hospice nurses rotate, but Dad's always happiest when Ed shows up. Dad asks him if the gauge of the railroad has changed. Doesn't this car seem wider than usual? In the middle of their conversation, Dad falls asleep.

Ed says this might be the beginning of the deep transition to active dying. Images of travel are typical. But saying that means nothing in terms of a timeline. We commit again to taking all of this one day at a time.

240

One of Dad's earliest memories is taking a train with Grandpa, his mother's father. A kind old man in a worn coat and fedora with a precocious, dark-eyed boy—they got star treatment from everyone on the line that connected small towns across northern Wisconsin. Dad can still name all the stops, with memories connected to each one.

For the years before he was old enough to go to school, he trailed Grandpa everywhere, a living shadow of the daughter the old man had lost. Then one day, sitting at the kitchen table, an argument erupted between Grandpa and his son-in-law: At the resurrection, would a person's body return as it was in peak health or in its state at death? This was a pressing question in the wake of World War I. Would the maimed come back whole? Would the gassed be able to see again?

Scripture was cited, but they couldn't agree and couldn't let it go. Dad remembers Grandpa fixing his hat low on his head, picking up his valise and walking stick, and vowing to never darken that door again. Grandpa was gone, and he kept his word.

When Dad tells of feeling abandoned as a child, he never mentions Grandpa, but soon enough some detail of this story floats into the conversation, usually with a barb about how little use he has for religion.

I think about the way Dad's stories weave through his history, revealing and obscuring it. I stop short of thinking, *and that's why...* I can't take the measure of anyone's wounds except (maybe) my own.

241

He's still fiercely dismissive of wearing a brief. He uses the urine bottle but increasingly misses the mark. Most of the time he falls asleep, and it all comes out then.

In a larger institution, this wouldn't be tolerated. It routinely creates extra, unpleasant work for Ali, and he vaguely knows that. He sometimes tries to help, which usually spreads the mess. One day he wraps a hard turd in a tissue, deposits it in the tissue box, then jokes to Ali, "Be careful. There's a gift in there..."

Should we urge him to wear a brief? It's Ali's decision. She sees how the idea of adult diapers crushes him. Ali sees his resentment and considers how it might work against his cooperation with other care. If she forces this issue, will his paranoia resurge? Is it worth the risk?

In the end, she chooses to preserve his dignity of mind, though it means more mess for her to clean up. I buy more underpads. More wipes. More sheets. Ali's a saint.

242

He says, "That Ali is amazing!" I agree.

He says he had a dream that he was on a conveyor belt moving out a delivery chute. The belt was sending things (including him) out too fast, and she rescued him. She had a magic key that slowed it down, then even reversed its direction.

243

Dad sometimes dreams of Mom as they were when they first knew each other, young and him wanting her, her holding him off until their wedding night but (he assures me) as excited as he was to take that next step.

He wakes at 2 a.m., calls Ali and tells her that he needs to meet Adele for breakfast.

244

Dad wants to reconnect with his first sweetheart, June, a summer romance after sixth grade. He had held her hand for the duration of a drive-in movie projected onto white sheets strung across the width of a smalltown Main Street. They were squeezed together in the backseat of a crowded car. The romance ended because her family moved away. They exchanged a few letters, but life moved on.

He wants me to look her up. I find her obituary. He's not surprised but wonders why he hadn't tried to call her the last time he was back in Wisconsin.

"What would Mom have thought about that?"

He lets out a soft "hmmm" and looks at me from under his eyebrows. We both know she would've been jealous, and he would've paid for it with a bout of her wounded silence.

In the middle of the night, Ali finds him sitting on the side of his bed. He says he's ready to go to an event at his high school.

He asks me to bring the yearbook pictures of his high school girlfriends, especially the one who broke his heart. He doesn't talk about it, but he's clear about her effect on him. He loved hard and early and suffered for it.

245

When Dad mentions "the one that got away" he means the muskie that boiled up in a fishing hole where he'd dropped a line. He was eight? Or nine? His dad was with him. They saw the size of the dorsal fin and knew it was huge, one of those old-timers that survived by lurking in the weeds.

Dad's father wasn't a patient man, and he soon tired of waiting for what might happen at the end of someone else's fishing pole. Dad says he vowed to come back on his own, but by that time his father's bragging gave some locals the idea of getting that fish with a stick of dynamite.

Dad mourned the loss of the chance at that fish. No battle of wits and patience. No sportsmanlike fair fight. Nothing that makes a man.

246

Dad has taught Ali to make poached eggs the way he likes them best. Each day, he nudges her a little—yolks too runny or too hard. Each day is a test, until one day something in him changes.

Ali brings the plate to the tray over his bed. He watches as she cuts through the white. The yolk oozes out, and she asks, "Do the eggs look perfect?"

He gazes at her and says, "If not, we see with imperfect eyes." The eggs are much the same as they've been for weeks.

247

Dad falls in love with Ali. She says every elderly man she's ever cared for has fallen in love with her. It's what old men do. It's not about her as much as a twilight urge, wanting to want, dabbling in the chemical thrill of love running in the veins.

He knows Ali's married, but he's convinced he can wait that out. "I'm next in line," he tells me with a smile. He dreams about taking her fishing (an intimate compliment). He starts eating three eggs for breakfast because, he says, "Eggs are good for—" and points to his groin.

He says a woman (Ali, he suspects) is crawling into his bed to sleep with him. He laboriously turns himself around to get a look at the woman's face. But, he says, by the time he turns around (sometimes head-to-toe in the bed) she's gone. All that's there is the pillow that braces his back.

Ali plays along, not taking his courtly charm seriously but not belittling it either. She knows that it's another way he's longing for more life. It's easy to see how vulnerable an old, besotted man would be with a less ethical caregiver.

Michelle tells me that she sees this again and again with men in hospice. She says it's also common for the kids to resent him for it. Some see their dying father reaching for love as a betrayal of their mother's memory.

This is no betrayal. His love for Adele still flows in him, but now love seeks a new place to land.

248

A different self emerges. He's less combative. Less concerned with being in control. His brittle pride is softening. He seems more curious. Love is in the mix, holding fear at bay.

The computer password he chose as a university student on the GI Bill was LOVE, a fact that struck me odd as a kid. What a strange gift (but not implausible) that the spiky parts fall away while love persists.

249

He's on another train journey. He looks out his windows, to the east and south across the valley. "What is this place?" he asks me. He's glad to be visiting here. If he were younger, he thinks he'd settle out here.

I tell him that when he was younger he *did* settle out here. He's surprised and pleased by that.

And I'm pleased that his desire for this place welling up out of a delusion is so fully reflected in the life he's led. This in contrast to Mom's too-late irritation over how she came to live in a place with no sidewalks.

250

Another step in decline. He needs help eating, seems to have some trouble swallowing. He holds his right hand drawn closer to his chest, a bit clawlike.

251

He asks me how long it took me to get over giardia, an intestinal parasite that wrought havoc with my guts in late summer 1979. I got it from eating dodgy food overseas, but it was also common among local hikers who drank from streams contaminated with feces.

I'm surprised he remembers this brief incident. What brought it to mind? He says he was helping some ranchers with their irrigation, and he was thirsty. He took a few sips of water straight from the stream, though he knew he shouldn't. He wants to remember the treatment he'll need if he starts to feel sick.

252

Does he know he's dying? He doesn't lack knowledge. He's just lived through Mom's decline. Before that, he knew from farm and military experience how animals and people die. But now, instead of dwelling in the end of things, he's found a particular angle of denial that allows him to dream and desire even more fiercely.

He's not mourning Mom anymore. Grief over yesterday has no place in his plans for today and tomorrow. In his few waking hours, he reminds me of a kid who doesn't want to go to sleep—that restless expectation that as soon as he does, all the good stuff will happen.

I wonder if this is, in part, the blind faith in his own immortality that shored him up through his military career. One day he talked with contempt about a fellow navigator who had no confidence in his own calculations. "He was a danger to himself and everyone he flew with!" If you're going to fly, you have to believe in your ability to go the distance into unknown territory and come home safely. Leave the worry to the ones on the ground, the waiting wives and kids.

253

Siblings cycle through. Last words. I'm glad when they're gone. Dad makes such an effort when they're here, and after they leave he collapses. Today he worries about snakes under his bed. Ali has put a potted lemon tree in his room, and he says he sees small animals circling around it. He doesn't want them to crawl up into his bed and bite his ankles.

Focus and poise are fragile. Disturbing the delicate routine we've cobbled together always has a cost.

254

Dad says in a conspiratorial voice, "Someone spilled the beans … but it wasn't me." I ask him who spilled the beans, but he says his lips are sealed. What did they tell that shouldn't have been told? He's silent. He's not the one who spilled the beans.

This is on his mind for several days. The thought won't let him go.

Then, in one moment of relief, he drops the secret. One fact from the Vietnam years. A secret that mustn't be shared and also can't be kept. A thing that can't be spoken of openly and also won't die in silence.

Dad once told me about how, when he was a boy, his father told him stories about dodgy things he'd done—poaching deer, working a bar during Prohibition—then swore him to secrecy. A bond between father and son. Dad hated knowing these things, but he kept silent.

Now, Dad's unsettled conscience binds me, and I feel how a shared secret casts another line of connection between us. Now I carry it, whether gift or burden or simply a sign of intimacy and trust. It had haunted him for days and, after one brief sentence tossed by him and caught by me, will never be spoken of again.

255

Dad is fixated on the idea of being young in the wilderness, hunting, fishing, trapping, frogging around in creeks. He lives in these images, part memory, part fantasy. He's not going quietly, but he doesn't seem to be raging against anything either. He seems to be reaching for some elemental pulse.

Nurse Ed advises me that at some point I should have a conversation with Dad about the fact that he's dying. But how to do that? He's not lacking signs. If he doesn't want to know, nothing I say will matter.

But I try. Delicately, I ask him if he has a sense of what's going on in his body.

"No."

I say it seems like his body is trying to let go, even as his mind speeds up. He's been so busy all his life maybe he can't even imagine what it means to slow down?

"I suppose so."

I say that can't be very comfortable.

"No, it's not."

His clipped replies make clear he doesn't want more talk like this. Ali comes into the room, and I repeat these things, so we all hear it. In Ali's presence, he gives me that sly smile that tells me he's humoring me, and then gazes deeply into her eyes. He's not going anywhere while this love drug makes his heart beat a little faster.

The love that fills this room now isn't a red paper cutout sold once a year in February. It isn't stuffed teddy bears and MWAH kissing emojis or the stuff found in swooning romance novels. It's not the easy obligatory sign-off on calls and cards. It's something else.

It's not domesticated and doesn't answer to bureaucracy. Forceful, pulsing, light and thick, singular and deeply entwined. The beat of this body's life, uncompromising and constantly spinning, fools the primal imagination into believing that he stands at the center while the sun arcs around him. To be honest, it terrifies me.

256

Aunt Florence spent weeks in the liminal space between breath and no breath. Her body was failing, her spirit was having otherworldly encounters, and her conscious mind held the status quo.

Finally, it became undeniable. She looked out her picture window at a profusion of just-opened apple blossoms. From her second floor view, she was eye level with the limbs that would be heaviest with fruit. "Aren't they beautiful!" she said, then asked with a little surprise in her voice, "Am I dying?" That began days of wrapping her mind around what it means to say goodbye.

One of her hospice workers gave me an image I return to: In this phase of dying, mind, body, and ineffable parts disentangle from each other, like strands of a rope unraveling. Each part proceeds to the exit at different rates. The goal of hospice is to help those parts "rhyme" at the end, each aspect completing its work before the body ends all possibility.

Dad still refuses the idea that he's dying. He doesn't want to hear about it from me. Maybe he'll listen to Ed, a fellow former military man helping him to understand new orders.

257

I sit on the wood pile by the red woodshed, barn cat poised by tall grass and waiting for movement. A good place to let a few tears go.

What's coming? The destination is indisputable, but how will he get there? Impossible to know. And it's always been impossible, but the illusion of continuity has been so strong. Now we see perceptible change, breaking the sense that this will go on forever.

With this phase, there'll be a new slate of decisions. New forking paths with no guarantees. *C'est la vie*, Dad would say with a shrug.

When this is over, I will have done all I could. That's extremely important to me. How else will I live with myself?

258

Agitation has returned with a new name: terminal restlessness. I recognize it from Florence's last weeks. A dying person will throw off all the covers, pick at their clothes, or undress in a literal stripping back of whatever weighs on them, even something as light as a pajama sleeve. Sometimes people become angry or violent, but that isn't Dad's path. Comfort medication can help restore calm, always the smallest dose possible to get there.

Ali tells me how she finds him sometimes—naked on the bed with all the covers on the floor, the tray table upended. He sometimes apologizes for making more work for her.

He knows what she goes through to hold indignities in check and preserve his sense of self, even now. And when that's impossible, her kindness fills the gap.

259

Ali tells a story about a resident in her past whose family refused comfort medication. The woman writhed and flailed through terminal restlessness for days. The family felt it was important for her to be medication-free so she could do what they believed was unfinished spiritual work. Ali had to follow their wishes but still winces at the painful memory of witnessing that suffering while physically holding the woman to keep her from hurting herself.

Nurse Ed hears this story and shakes his head. If someone is in that much discomfort, he says, they're not doing any spiritual work. The only work they're doing is withstanding the pain.

It's a gruesome and sad image. Pain is trauma, and these last days are a time for releasing whatever traces remain, not for taking on new wounds. For Dad, a minimal dose of anti-anxiety medication takes the edge off. He's less agitated, and he's able to sleep.

260

His body loses strength by the day. His mind is more calm. I feel it. I think it. I work through what more (if anything) I could be doing now for him.

One day I field a number of calls from friends wanting to catch up about work or life. I ask them all how they are, and they tell me, and I listen politely while screaming inside, *My father is dying! I don't give a fuck about your new kitchen cabinets!*

And my teeth grind when I hear them urge, "Are you taking care of yourself? Take care of yourself!" I know they mean well, but today it sounds like a trite line from a greeting card. Maybe that's as much as is possible across this divide between the sidelines and the bedside.

Few people want to spend time in the world where rhythms of death and dying dictate the hours, wondering about the threads that hold us together with our ancestors, the shape of a nose, the shape of a thought, a set of concerns, a worry over potatoes being harvested in time and then, days later in a different dream, planted on time.

261

He says, "We didn't see you for years, and now you're here every day."

"Yep," I say. It is so improbable.

The truth? I was away for those years finding the perspective and inner skills I would need to be useful here, now. I couldn't know then that this is where all that work would lead, but dumb luck sometimes points us in the direction we'd never choose on our own.

262

This afternoon I stand across the exposed undercarriage of a bale wagon. It looks like something Dr. Seuss would have drawn, with a seat perched out front and a collection of bent tubes, levers, and springs powering a chain drive that draws a hay bale up onto a platform that, when full, raises up to deposit a layer of bales into what eventually becomes a small stack. It's a mechanical answer to the lack of teenagers who want to buck bales.

A lever has broken. Several tubes have been unmoored from their network to make it possible to remove the broken pieces. That's done, the lever replaced, and now it can be put back together.

Les, architect of the repair and user of the machine, peers into the guts, following the various tubes to their conclusions, checking a mental list for what must be put back in place. So much ranch work is done alone, a private act measured only by outcome: Does the machine work as it should (or at least get the job done)?

His deft problem solving brings a lifetime of experience to bear and reminds me of Dad (what exactly is *he* puzzling through right now?). I ask Les small questions, not expecting that I'll learn how it all works but interested to hear how he explains it. I'm a distraction, but he humors my curiosity about breakdown and repair.

I stand by as witness, seeing dimly what he sees. Still, I hope for his success and lean with him toward the outcome, though only he will live with the results.

263

Vulnerability is a permanent condition for all of us, even (perhaps especially) when we're at the peak of our strength. I forget that—or pretend otherwise—at my peril.

264

Yet weaker by the day. Bowels are shutting down. He's too tired to chew toast, so now it's just eggs and canned pears on the breakfast plate, and much of that goes uneaten. We know he's done when he has to rest to gather enough strength to finish chewing what becomes the last bite.

265

Les asks if I have the court order that details how Dad and a neighbor share water in the little irrigation ditch. He suspects the neighbor will see Dad's decline as an opening to bend or break the terms.

I go to the county office and sit with the thick book of disputes for the creek where the water originates. "Whiskey is for drinking; water is for fighting over," wrote Mark Twain. An apt epigraph for a legal record full of people measuring what they think is owed them against the reality of a dynamic, unpredictable, and highly limited resource meant to be shared among a community of rights holders. It makes for some ridiculous arguments that read like toddler tantrums. The chasm between individual entitlement and collective responsibility is wide.

Every spring, people are invited to come out to a communal ditch cleaning day. Fewer people show up each year, and some of those just come to socialize. Les and one other fella go up the canyon to the main headgate to move boulders and shift fallen trees to turn the water in to the ditch. Dad used to do this, and he forbid me from going up. Too dangerous, he said. It's hard, necessary labor that marks the start of the growing season and yet guarantees nothing.

The water runs cold on even the hottest day. Snow melts on the weather's schedule, and when it's gone, the ditch will go dry until next year. A furious few months to make the most of it, irrigating hayfields and gardens and, increasingly, illegally filling decorative ponds.

I give Les a copy of the court order. In a few months, I'll have to remind the neighbor of the terms. He's not rid of Dad just yet.

266

Even after Florence had a heart attack and could barely stand, she never saw herself as diminished. The gap between her sense of self and the reality of her body simply puzzled her: "Why can't I live like I used to live?" "Who are all these people in my apartment, and why can't I tell them to leave?"

She'd always been in control of her life. Why couldn't she *decide* her way out of this, too? She could've written the script for her nephew.

267

Florence had been having waking dreams for more than a week. She had five days left, though none of us knew that.

A tray of food came, and she wanted nothing. She sighed, worn out, "Do I have to do this every day? Eat and drink?"

She described life prior to her heart attack as "up" and after as "down." She reflected, "This isn't how I imagined dying." How did she think it would be? "I thought everything would just go on like it was when things were up."

She thought for awhile, then got practical: "How do I do it? Do I just go to sleep?" I heard the awakening of an idea: If she couldn't will her previous health to return, did she need to will herself to die?

268

Nurse Ed sits by Dad's bedside. I sit in a chair to the side, out of Dad's line of vision.

Dad barely talks these days. His mouth may be silent, but his eyes roam and speak to anyone who can listen. He still takes a few bites of breakfast, but is that simply to please Ali?

Physical signs point to him being days or hours away from his last breath, but he still hasn't come around to the idea that he's dying. We could let him die in this state of mind, but dogged refusal seems at odds with everything else he's doing. He doesn't want to talk about it with me, so I've asked Ed.

Ed is both matter-of-fact and keenly sensitive. In his hands, being direct isn't brutal—it's a kindness. A few well-tuned sentences can help Dad over a hurdle Ed has seen many times over the years. At the same time, Ed reminds me that we don't know what it's like to die. What looks from the outside like a slowing into stasis may be anything but. I need to keep my own limited sight in mind.

Dad's listening. Ed tells him, in a couple of different ways, that he's dying. He'll be going to meet Adele soon. Will that be alright?

Two faint words: "That's okay." Dad slowly pulls one hand out from under the covers to clasp Ed's, an eloquent and monumental gesture given Dad's faded strength. Ed asks if he'd like to know more about what to expect in the coming days. It might help him feel more in control. A small nod.

Ed says that he may want to sleep more. He may not want to eat or drink anymore. He doesn't need to do anything. What's happening will happen on its own. His work is done.

They sit, hands clasped, in silence.

269

When he reaches for a glass, his hand misses by several inches off to the side. Is his vision changing?

No, a hospice nurse says. In this last phase, the body loses its orientation in space. This is normal. Part of the gradual withdrawal from physical existence.

I can't stop thinking about how it would feel for my body's physical boundaries to dissolve… skin no longer surface but sieve, myriad holes expanding into one another until the structure of sieve itself disappears. Ice melting into snow melting into water, shape giving way to flow.

He's perfectly calm. I can't see the flux he sees. What for me seems like a surreal collapse of self looks more like, for him, perhaps… a merging with everything else.

270

"How do you feel?" I get that question a lot.

I don't know. I feel something like an internal stretching. Like I'm taking a big inhale, lungs expanding by millimeters to get whatever extra capacity I need to face what's in front of me. Not run away or hide in false certainties. To gain what it takes to stay in this space of what can't be known.

<h1 style="text-align:center">271</h1>

He usually folds his hands over his abdomen. I like the feel of his soft fingers, the bony structures. I put a hand to his smooth forehead, over the sparse hair on the top of his head. He sleeps on. Peaceful.

But I'm not peaceful. Arrows over sibling nonsense poke me, always underneath it all some version of the old saw about who got the most love from the parents. And then my own impatience at myself: *Why am I thinking about that? Why am I giving that any attention in these last hours? Why am I stepping out of this expansive moment into that narrow, sullen rut?*

Michelle tells me that anger is a flash that lasts just seconds. After those seconds, if I stay angry it's because I've chosen it.

Anger is engagement. In families it can be a form of attachment. I remember that "hospice" and "hostility" share the same root. Can I hospice the part of me that's attached to that painful cycle? Or will I choose anger now?

I drag my attention back to him, matching my breath to his for minutes. I think about boundless love and how fraught its translation into daily action. How we long for the unconditional, infinite bond and expect that it can be fully satisfied by conditional, finite acts—an impossibility from the start. Yet I must try! Love imperfectly or not at all. There's always enough to go around, if I choose to see the world so.

272

Dad doesn't know me, but he trusts that I'm on his side. He holds my hand, says he's glad to see me, calls me his bodyguard, and tells me he loves me. I wish I'd seen more of this father all these years.

But we have right now and these few days (with their fewer waking hours) remaining. I tell him I hope to see him in my dreams. We both dream so much that we're bound to run into each other. He smiles at that.

273

As I stood vigil for Florence, staff and her neighbors sputtered through to say hello, meaning goodbye. We talked quietly in the living room, around the corner from Florence in her bed. They told me stories about her and often told me about their own experience losing a relative. A mother. A grandfather. A cousin.

It became clear that relating these stories was not for my benefit but for the teller's. And in my exhaustion, I didn't welcome it. I didn't want to listen to their grief, especially as I held my own in check.

But with one eye on Florence while I listened to people who cared about her, she reminded me to summon an ounce of her own immense patience. Stay in this moment. She reminded me, in her stillness, how little we allow ourselves to be with grief—our own or others'—in our smiles-and-lights-always-on culture.

I was holding my breath through it all. I needed to let myself breathe.

274

Grief feels selfish. *My* loss. *My* pain. It's so intimate. The rip and tear right at the parts that hold everything else together. Tendons turn to jelly.

But this grief isn't just mine. In the end, we all lose what we love. It's in the condition of things, right from the start. And this bare fact binds me to everyone else, no matter who.

275

Dad's navigating his last phase as Mom did, as a quiet and pain-free semi-sleep. Hospice nurses visit regularly. I've been advised that it's best not to hover, not to touch him in this last phase.

The dying may want our presence, but they aren't helped by us clinging to them, laying our unresolved selves on them like a heavy cloak, just at the moment they defy gravity. I sit by Dad but don't touch him. Just a light kiss on the forehead when I go.

276

He hasn't spoken for more than a day but looks at Ali—or looks through her?—and rasps, "I love you so much!" The next day, he goes, a half hour after Ali's usual morning check, a half hour before I usually arrive. He goes alone, in the morning—his favorite time of day—as is his choice.

I love you so much! Who or what did he mean by "you"?

Ali?

Adele?

Life itself?

Does knowing matter? Whatever its object, the sheer feeling of being in love must've filled his body to overflowing. How else would he have summoned the strength for those last words? What a gift at any time of life. But at the end? There are worse ways to go.

Ali, a hospice nurse, and I dress him in a fresh work shirt and jeans for the spring season, with red suspenders, pocketknife, bandana in his back pocket, and the boots he'd wear to irrigate the pasture.

I sit with him some hours, his body giving up the last of its heat. Another long, singular exhale. Then I hear his voice in my ear: *Don't be morbid. Get a move on!*

Attend

278

Dad dies in the midst of spring cleanup. In his last weeks, after our morning visit, I went to the ranch to trim overgrowth and chuck fallen limbs onto the ditch banks. The day after he dies, the water that had been turned in far up the mountain finally reaches the ranch, washing down pine needles and dead leaves. They need to be cleared. Today.

Grief is physical. Grief is work. There's nothing to do about it, but bearing it—holding it without refusing it—is something I had to learn. I was in my late twenties when my business partner Howard was murdered. A sudden lesson in ripping absence. I became a proxy widow, running our business, helping to sort out his apartment and hold a memorial service, all while running from the unthinkable wrongness of it all. Whether I could think it or not, it was done.

Back then, I held grief in my head. It seeped into my bones and calcified. Now, I pull on knee-high waterproof boots and stumble down the ditch's uneven sand and rock bottom, stabbing at debris with a pitchfork, clearing accumulated leaves that dam the flow, crying. I can't hear myself over the babble of clear, cold water rushing around my boots.

Dad loved this time of year when life bursts after months of hibernation. For more than a decade, he hadn't had the balance to be down in the ditch doing what I do now. I walk in his steps.

The ponderosa pine cones and needles fallen around the house need to be raked up. That was Mom's work. I walk in her footsteps, too.

279

When Howard's best friend was dying of AIDS, I visited him only once, at a gathering with dozens of people. Fred's usual big smile floated above his withered body. I'm sure I went to his bedside (it's the polite thing to do), but I don't remember what I said. I'm sure he was gracious, because that's the person he was. And I'm guessing he saw the fear in me. Not fear of AIDS (though that was so common in the 1980s, people afraid to touch or hold or kiss) but fear of more loss, more darkness once again stepping into the room to grab me by the throat.

Another friend died in the hospital of a slow rolling health crisis. There was time for me to visit her. I didn't go.

Cowardly. *Why was I so paralyzed? Why did I hold myself away?*

I couldn't fix them, and I didn't know the right thing to say. I felt useless.

It didn't seem enough to simply be with them and show them how I felt about our friendship. It took years to realize that being with them would've been enough. Simply sitting with them, sharing a look or the pressure of our hands together, would've been enough.

Competence and confidence aren't the same as care. To attend and witness are ways we accompany each other even when one is going where the other can't follow. Acts that don't seem like acts at all but are, in fact, a well of quiet enoughness.

280

A few weeks before he died, Dad announced that I got the Allbaugh nose, a feature of his mother's family. I know I have his mother's face. A portrait of her as a young teen shows that. When he saw me from across the yard last summer, he said the shape of my body reminded him of his aunt, who raised him after his mother died. I look in the mirror and see his cheekbones.

Mom's brother told me that I remind him of their mother, my Swedish grandmother who was never one for lavishing hugs and "I love you" but showed her affection in actions. Florence told me I have the spirit of her mother, who bravely came alone from Norway on a ship, speaking no English.

Am I some shadow cast by an accumulation of ancestors, their attitudes and biological proclivities, their traumas and desires all come to rest in me, asking, *What will you say on our behalf? What will you do to keep us alive?*

281

Les knocks on the door of the ranch house. He has a question.

He points out a pile of treated lumber that Dad bought to build a diversion for the ditch. The diversion would raise the water level at an outtake, so the far field could be better irrigated and improve the hay crop. A good plan, but the lumber sat. Les had asked Dad a couple times whether he could build it for him. No.

Why did Dad refuse? Les thinks Dad bought the lumber just as his vision or tremor became bad enough to knock his confidence. If his measurements weren't right or the corners not tight, the built frame would turn out wonky. Or maybe he wasn't sure he could install it, climbing in and out of the ditch, wrestling it into place. Embarrassing. Infuriating. Damaged pride. Some early loss of his own capabilities, alongside what was unfolding in the house with his wife.

Do I mind if Les builds it? I hear in his offer a tribute. He's grieving his friend, too.

Yes, I say. Build it. Finish what he couldn't.

282

Dad opted for cremation and wanted no marker because, he said, he didn't want to give anyone a chance to piss on his grave. He had a friend who'd done that to someone else, going to the cemetery in some off hour. He delighted in his friend doing it but didn't much like the idea of anyone doing it to him. He'd rather his elements be scattered and nourish the soil, which was more in keeping with his ethos anyway.

283

I emerge from this tunnel of decline and dying and look out at the world. Where did all the angry people come from? What are they so angry about? Their bad faith arguments are no clue, except that they seem to vent some unseen wound. They seem to nurture grievance in their belly. They seem to enjoy spreading their anger around.

What fear, sadness, or grief might speak if those emotions weren't considered weakness? If the soft belly of vulnerability wasn't armored up with contempt and sarcasm? Is that a gargling of unresolved ruptures?

I can't speak with it through the volume of noise. I can't get there, and I can't see a point to standing in its path. Today, I wave it past. Tomorrow, we'll see.

284

In the center of the labyrinth, some people put a token of a thing they want to leave behind—or a thing that left them behind. They walk the path to the center and set down an object that represents their grief, trauma, loss, love, or longing. A seashell. A photo. A school ID card. A ring. A necklace. Ashes. A small skull made from clay. A heart made from wood. A Santa figurine. A toy truck. A letter written to a son on what would've been his sixteenth birthday. A letter-to-self lamenting the damage she'd done. An empty bourbon bottle. An empty cigarette pack. A piggy bank. A playing card.

After Patty died, the labyrinth itself took on an aura of grief. The objects were left to accumulate, a bricolage of whatever was too much to carry among the growing crowd of people struggling with what needed to be laid down.

After a few years, the layer upon layer of stuff felt overwhelming. It became a chaotic pile of stories that weren't being released but instead held, to be revisited by their authors and wondered over by others. Some walkers arrived at the center and felt the weight. "Heavy," one woman declared, shaking her head.

The labyrinth had become a shrine. It's not really what a labyrinth is for. The labyrinth is an architecture not for *hanging on* but for *moving through.*

I talked this over with Helmut. Because of my proximity, I was gradually becoming the labyrinth's caretaker. He agreed that we could respectfully remove the objects and restore the labyrinth as an experience, not a destination. The objects' work was done, and the path could again be a neutral invitation for everyone.

That bothered some people, the ones I imagine who'd left personal items or decorations that read like a silent declaration: *I was here.* Inside that impulse, I read questions: *Do you see me? Does anyone feel what I feel?* And behind those a more basic question: *Do I matter?*

I see them. I wonder about them. I read the notes left behind, sometimes look for obituaries online, and watch the wind pick up ashes someone's scattered, carrying them farther than before, though possibly not far enough.

In the end, Dad gave up anger and grudges in favor of love. I tell a neighbor, a man who knew my dad as a no-nonsense rancher, about this progression. How Dad, at the age of 92, finally laid down this crusty exterior for, of all things, love.

He listens, pauses, then says quietly, "It's just too bad it took him that long to get there."

Yes. But he got there in the end.

286

They ushered me in. I ushered them out. An imperative of mutual care. There is something that needs to be addressed. Something ineffable, though "spirit" and "soul" are so freighted with meaning and associations that I can't use them.

Still, something ineffable. I make no claim about its nature or location. Does it survive the body? I don't know. Are its manifestations a specter from another realm or a trick of neurobiology that attends the end? I don't know.

What I can say is that it emerges in the dark, this other-than mode of being. Something aside from conscious thought. Something to be respected but not a puzzle to be decoded. Maybe a kind of dreaming.

I know what I witnessed, but I won't claim that it proves anything about what comes after the last breath. I don't know, and I don't want to pretend that I do.

I don't mind sitting with the mystery, those uncanny, undomesticated moments that beg description but answer only to a shrug and nod of respect. I can't brush them aside, and I won't pin them down like a dead butterfly in a collector's box. It's enough for me that I was in the room with them. It is. They are. I am.

287

We got lucky. So lucky. We mostly escaped the traps of intense, interventionist medical care when what was needed was a slower, hands-on approach. Acute gave way to chronic. Quantity of days gave way to quality of life. Demands for efficiency gave way to patience.

Mom's ER doctor, whose own mother had Alzheimer's, had already thought deeply about appropriate treatment for people with dementia.

Neither Mom nor Dad were in acute physical pain. Managing pain would've severely altered the path we followed.

The impulse to talk over a tractor repair took Les to the house soon after Dad fell, saving him hours of pain and possibly his life.

The hospice center and field service were staffed with kind, grounded, experienced, knowledgeable, generous professionals. People I know in other parts of the country haven't always had such good hospice providers.

Mom moved out of the licensed nursing home just weeks before COVID lockdowns. The early lockdown protocols were understandably strict for nursing homes. But I'm grateful not to be haunted by the image of her dying disoriented and disconnected, confined to her room without family visits or even hospice support, her only human connection a sputter of anonymous gowned-and-masked figures coming and going, rushing, always rushing, to care for all the people living and dying on the long hallways. She didn't, but many did.

288

For three years, I had gauged my energy to reach Dad's last breath, exhausting everything, knowing that after he was dressed, the funeral home called, his room cleared, and his obituary written, my effort would be done. A sibling was named as executor of Dad's will. I could go home and crawl into my bed for a month or more to sleep and grieve.

A week later, the sibling drops out. I need to see the estate to its end, too. I crawl out of my bed, find a lawyer, and begin a very different chapter of family obligation, wounded yet walking. I was into a crush of paperwork and legalities—the will, probate, court dates, taxes, accounts, auctions, household goods, assessments, real estate. Months of making inventories of the house and ranch buildings, sorting what can be sold from what is only fit for trash or the burn pile.

Les will need time to move his herd elsewhere, but not so soon after calving and not so soon before haying. Another season will need seeing to.

289

On a clear morning, I see Les rushing from the pasture. A cow has rolled onto her back for no good reason. It happens, and it's a quick way to die. He's getting the tractor and slings and hay bales to right her, maybe in time for her lungs to clear the fluid that accumulates. She may be able to walk away.

A neighbor comes to help. For hours they boost and bolster her sagging weight. I hover, staying out of the way but near enough to run for whatever they might need, until afternoon when Les has to tend his irrigation or risk flooding out the neighbors. I tell him I'll stay with her. I stand, feet planted, bracing her head to keep it from swaying. Some time later, her eyes turn to glass.

I call Les, and when he returns, he seems to sag. He apologizes. He didn't mean for me to bear that. *But why not?* I think. *This is part of what happens in this place. I'm here, so why should I be sheltered from it?* And that's not even important now. The cow's four-day-old calf sleeps nearby in the shade. He's hungry, and she needs to be buried, a sober need to attend to what lives even as the dead occupy our minds.

We herd the calf to the corral, and Les goes out to finish afternoon chores. I find a calf bottle Dad kept from his years of necessity and warm up the little milk I have in the fridge. Les feeds the calf, and I offer to make the twice-daily bottles if he wants to raise it.

We move the cow to the secluded spot near where, years before, Dad buried the well-loved Jersey milk cow, put down when she became too old to stand and crows began to peck at her. The neighbor will come later to help Les bury what is no longer a cow but a carcass, as a body becomes a corpse.

The shift in terms marks the fundamental change from the life that sustained itself to what remains to be addressed by those who remember. The corpse and carcass go back to the earth they came from, where they first found form, unexpectedly, through a coupling, planting, and amniotic nurturing, fed by the eating, drinking, ruminating life of a mother until expelled to the first bawling breath.

The next morning, Les brings a sack of powdered milk replacer. This routine of feedings, 6 a.m. and 6 p.m., will see me through the rest of spring and summer, forcing me out of bed on mornings I wake as glass—brittle, stiff, and ready to shatter.

Only later do I realize that Les likely would've preferred to sell the calf outright. I'm not sure the effort and expense of hand raising a calf passes muster on a balance sheet. But Les saw what I couldn't, that in my offer to take on the calf's daily routine, I was reaching for what's alive and ongoing, a counterweight to the daily audit of all that had stopped, been lost, or gone missing. A kindness I appreciated only after months of watching the calf grow and find his place in a small herd that made space for an orphan.

290

Every relationship carries, from its very beginning, the fact that one of us will die first. One of us will have to mourn and bear witness to the loss of the other.

And yet, mourning doesn't come naturally. It's easier to leave it to the professionals. The funeral director. The religious figures. But mourning is everyone's work. Sometimes we're undone by it, and why shouldn't we be? If we aren't, how deeply did we actually love? Did we really care, or were we transacting some business?

We are broken. And then our entanglements with other people and creatures and things that need doing bring us back to something like life. Not the same as it was. There is no going back. But there is *now*, and soon a *next* shows itself.

But first we have to stop running from the chasm that opened up where someone we love used to be. First we have to sit on the edge of that abyss and remember them, their stories, their love of us, our love of them, as well as the arguments we had and especially the arguments we didn't have, the things left unsaid or willfully misremembered. The practice of loving, unfinished and all.

291

I clean out a desk drawer where Mom stashed things. Things that worked in their day and she kept because *you never know*—they might still be useful for the person who's resourceful enough:

broken scissors
several halves of crayons
crumbling pink erasers
a loose aspirin, dirty around the edges
crisp rubberbands
rusted paperclips
dried out felt tip markers
empty ballpoint pens
one loose staple
a screw
a bobby pin
one jigsaw puzzle piece

292

They're not alive, but they still *are*. How do I describe them now?

They are *decedents*. The legal term for their new state of being.

They are *deceased*. I use that word when I close accounts and ask organizations to take them off mailing lists. It's bureaucratic. It says, *I need your help, not your sympathy.*

I never describe them as *departed*, a word that has the sound of funeral oratory by a too-serious preacher in a church my parents would never have attended.

They aren't my *late* parents. They'd never be late for anything, even their own deaths.

Some say they've *transitioned*, a pillowy word that points to a cosmology of comfort. It works for some, and when they use it I don't argue, but I also don't agree.

I sometimes say, *they've found their way to another plane.* It gestures to the intangible but for me also echoes with the precise mathematics of flying Dad so loved.

I don't say they're *gone,* which always begs the question, *gone where?* For that I have no answer except in the physical realm.

Sometimes *dissolved* comes to mind. That feels accurate, materially. Their wet parts evaporated. The chemical bonds that made structure, shape, colors, hardness, and softness all fell apart.

Mom's literary mind may have preferred *deliquesced.*

Dad may have preferred *rendered*, a farm word I learned after the first hog was butchered and he showed us how to make lard and cracklings.

In my own mind, I prefer the thud of a single syllable: *dead*. It's a word that pulls no punches. It gets to the stopped heart of the matter.

293

However I describe them, I can't get away from using a word of being. The memory of them, their trail of documents, the ghost I see in a gesture I make—they *were* and still *are*.

Their strands of mind, body, and the ineffable have permanently unraveled. Maybe this is why I describe this phase as *unwinding* fifty years of my parents' life on a ranch. *Clearing out* sounds too sudden. *Cleaning up* too clinical. *Unwinding* describes the spirals of effort I'll make over the coming year, mostly by hand, sometimes on my knees.

Les offers to speed the process of loading scrap metal into the big recycler container. His tractor will make short work of it, but I tell him I'm okay unpicking the piles piece by piece. He watches me sorting and hefting and observes, "You need to say goodbye to every piece, doncha."

I didn't realize it until he said it. It's a way to work through another layer of sedimented feeling.

And with more speed, I would've missed the tin can that Dad used to carry things (a screwdriver, a little hardware) when one hand was busy with his walking stick. He'd added a thin wire handle to make it easy to carry. It's the same size of tin can that, in Hawaii, he would turn upside down, punch two holes into the sides across the diameter, and attach a handle of cotton rope. Two of those made good stilts for a five-year-old.

294

My cold toes have something to say today. The twinge in my shoulders from yesterday's work speaks. The wrist I broke when I fell off a horse at age eleven aches. Now, an electric buzz in my veins. Sleeplessness? Worry over all that's yet to be done? Knowledge is made and felt in every part of the body.

295

In the winter after he's gone, I wear the parka shell from Dad's early 1950s winter survival training. I pull down his Stormy Kromer hat to keep my ears warm. I wear a thick flannel shirt and insulated canvas pants he handed down to me the first winter after I came back. That saved me spending money on winter clothes. I was surprised that they fit. It's become something of a uniform, and I stay warm walking the labyrinth at zero degrees.

In summer, I use a set of his tools and the pocketknife he gave me as a birthday present soon after I came back. "Do you have a pocket-knife? You need a pocketknife." I push his red wheelbarrow out to the labyrinth to haul away weeds and trimmings from the prolific bushes and vines.

I have Mom's bags of quilting scraps. I spend a summer and fall making patchworks that will keep me and others warm in the winter. As the scraps dwindle, I add in fabrics from my own stash. Gradually, the quilts take on a color palette closer to my own taste. But there's always a bit of her in there. Blue, her favorite color, will always be hers.

Mom is more likely to show up in my dreams. There, Dad is absent. I think of them both when pairs of Canada geese fly past the labyrinth, moving from one pond to the next. And when quail scratch for sunflower seeds scattered on the back porch. Mated for life and on the move.

296

I dream.

"What's the square root of two?" a figure asks.

"I am."

297

A voicemail on my phone goes unheard. It's from Dad, calling me in from the field to the house for lunch. A couple hours later, Mom had a stroke. I imagine his reedy tone and no-nonsense ask. I can't listen to it, and I can't delete it. An artifact I leave unearthed.

Twenty-five years after I last heard my business partner's voice, a researcher unearthed a film that included an interview with him. It was made in the years I first knew Howie. I watched the film, and there he was talking, tilting his head, leaning forward to make a point. Watching him, it was so familiar I could barely breathe. I studied his every gesture, anticipating the last shot and that shock of loss that's buried in me to surface all over again.

And then he laughed—a distinctive laugh that condensed everything I love about him into one gust of air. And through tears I laughed, too.

Other absences crowd in, other people gone too soon, swells of what might have been (and relief for some that wasn't). There is no looking back that isn't also a moving forward (though tiny whiplash reversals can feel like standing still). I miss him. I miss them.

I mull over what I can remember, mangled pieces of their particularities. I try to remember their voices, gestures, and quirks. I wonder what they might say. What things they might make. The books or movies or TV shows they might recommend. What jokes they might tell me. What new ideas they might lob my way. The way they might urge me to get on with my own particularity.

Surprise me, I want to say to them. *Surprise us,* they say back.

298

About a week before she died, Florence said I might find among her things a large brown envelope marked "Do Not Open." She couldn't remember where she'd hidden it. She might have already gotten rid of it. She said that, if I found it, I should destroy it. She didn't want to forget what it held (thus the envelope), and she didn't want it remembered (thus the instruction).

What could be in that envelope? As I watched Florence doze, the question floated light among the weightier facts in the room. Given her quiet life and exceeding modesty, I imagined love letters, perhaps from the one she called "the love of my life." Undoubtedly handwritten in cursive with a fountain pen. (They hadn't married because his mother felt Florence's scoliosis made her unfit to have children. In the late 1920s, no doctor disagreed.)

I gave up the search after the last piece of furniture in her small apartment was accounted for, all her belongings boxed and distributed. Was it there to be found? Did I miss it? Or had she already destroyed its body, if not its memory?

Still, the envelope found me. Curiosity about finding gave way to frustration at *not* finding, then disappointment and letting go, shifting expectation from *might have been* to *never will be*. Then, unexpectedly, silent grief for the idea of a secret so urgent that it cannot be forgotten and yet must not be remembered. And out of that, a hum of newer curiosity and fuller fascination. Not the envelope she hid but the one she willed me.

299

The rupture between body and body won't be bridged, as much as reminiscence and dreams and psychics try. What is mourning doing in that fractured space? What story is it telling through the grip on my mind and mood? What can it possibly say to explain how one world collapses and another goes on?

In the early days after Howie's murder, I'd wake up in the before-world where he was still breezing into the office with a new joke. For a few seconds, all was as it should be. Then wakefulness opened up the black hole where he should've been (how can a hole be so heavy?).

This mourning is less jarring. And I know now that mourning is ongoing, a background murmur and reminder that losing is something we all do, from our first breath. It binds us together, our common thread.

300

Seven months after Dad died, I'm nearly done clearing up the ranch. It's part of fifteen months of living at the ranch taking care of Lady and the barn cat, going about the routines and one-offs of tending to what's dissolving.

The house is clean and empty except for my nomadic bits and pieces. The farm equipment (the good stuff and the graveyard) is gone. I'm beyond weary of sleeping on the old twin bed I'd moved into the living room during the early days when it seemed possible that Dad would come home, heal up, and go on for as many more years as he could muster. I want to sleep in my own bed again, at the apartment up the hill I've barely inhabited for the past year.

Lady has warmed to me, sometimes nudging for a scratch behind her ears or flopping down for hip and shoulder massage. She's become incontinent, so we take a midnight walk around the yard. Waterproof underpads used on both Mom's and Dad's bed at West Hills now come in handy for her bed. But she's wise to the ways I hide incontinence medication in her food or a bit of peanut butter. That's hit and miss.

The formerly-feral barn cat can't be left behind and won't be an easy fit anywhere. She's used to roaming over acres of territory and is highly suspicious of people. Over the last few years we've become friends. With some adjustment on both our parts, the cat could live with me. But what about Lady?

I consult the veterinarian who's cared for all the ranch animals. He was a good friend to Dad, empathetic and thoughtful, quick when it's kind and slow when it's needed. He says Lady's people are gone. She's 18 years old—a long life for a dog. She's had a good summer. The coming winter will be hard on her. Her incontinence will only get worse.

It seems unkind to re-home her to a new place she doesn't know. The practicalities of bringing her to live with me are impossible. He says that if I feel it's time to say goodbye, I should say that with no guilt. He gives me ethical permission to put her to sleep, but that's not the same as moral license. What *must* be done does not automatically become what we *want* to do.

Nevertheless.

Nevertheless, I do. And bury her in a patch of hundreds of lodgepole pines I helped to plant in the early 1970s, soon after we moved to Montana. Row after row, Dad drove a shovel into the sandy soil and pushed the handle away from him, opening up a space in the earth. Into this gap I stuck a spindly sapling. I remember thinking it was a waste of time. *How could these fragile things possibly grow?*

Fifty years later, not only have they grown, some have fallen and decayed and made a rich patch for elk that come to bed down or calve. Deer travel through, and wild turkeys roost. Dad's previous hunting dog, who died of old age in a nest of hay nearly forty years ago, is buried here. Then, Dad got down into the large hole he'd dug for her, and from the lip I helped him lower her burlap-covered body. It was one of the few times I ever saw him cry.

Now, I get down into the grave I've dug for Lady, placing her burlap-wrapped body at the bottom, then climb out and fill it in with rock and sand. She's there with handfuls of Mom's and Dad's ashes in the quietest, wildest place on the ranch, which really isn't all that quiet or wild anymore, increasingly surrounded on all sides by houses and the neighbor's Sunday shooting practice.

I feel it in my marrow. Tears that haven't come for Mom or Dad come for their dog. During and after their care, I'd been preoccupied with all the clear-eyed decisions I needed to make. *Grieve later,* I told myself. Now, it's later.

301

When logic said it was time to say goodbye, when I had no more in me to give, a scrap of me still wondered if there was anything more I could've done for Lady. Time after time in the previous years I'd hit what seemed like a problem with no solution or just one wretched solution. And after turning it over and over, suddenly, the surprise of a new idea. A sideways thought that might be a new approach. It didn't always work out, but it was usually worth a try.

We invent what we need, and when nothing new comes, what *is* has to be enough. I felt again that spiraling thought that churned in those last months first with Mom and then Dad. *What more is possible? What have I overlooked or not yet thought?*

The vet advised me not to feel guilty. Lady was treated with dignity and loving care. She wasn't in pain. All things I told myself, an echo of the hospice workers who said similar things about both Mom and Dad. We did our best for them, and it's not too much to say that each experienced a good death.

302

I hear myself saying over dinner with neighbors that I'll always feel regret about putting the dog down. I know it was the right decision, but I wish there could've been another way. I wish she could've died in her sleep. I wish her body had chosen the moment to leave. That timing wasn't to be. Let me say that again: *I'll always regret that I had to make that decision.*

That regret embodies the grief of a loved being's going, the weight of responsibility for their care, the always-uncertain nature of how things proceed and might've been. I don't torture myself with it, and I don't consider it a thing to get over. That regret is recognition that alongside any decision are other paths not taken. Other possibilities that went unthought. Sometimes "good" has to be good enough, but I can still hold a horizon of "better."

I say this at a dinner table, and in an irritating chorus, the others say, "No! You shouldn't feel that way!" And then one, like a self-help meme come to life, says, "They let us know when they're ready to go." And under that suffocating statement—a comfort to them, a too-easy summing up to me—I change the subject.

For days that phrase came back to me. *They let us know when they're ready to go.*

As if signs are crystal clear in the zone between being and not-being, a zone that can last an instant or years.

As if we can always distinguish between the signs that we sense from loved ones and the signs that are actually our own interests projected outward, too terrible to own yet longing to be seen.

As if we can hear clearly the contradictory, shifting messages of mind, body, and ineffable parts unfurling toward the exit at different rates. *Is that the body screaming for release while the mind doggedly clings to life? Is that the mind already gone while the body continues to tick over like a well-wound clock? Is that the ineffable despairing while the other parts cling to ongoingness?*

They let us know… Across the divide between the one who is going and the witness-caregiver, the static can be immense. It's tempting to hear what we *want* to hear. It's easy to forget that we're always limited by what our inner capacities *allow* us to hear. Because what we allow ourselves to hear can become something we may need to act on—to take action we'd rather not bear—to take action we can only bear through an unconditional commitment to doing what's necessary out of lovingkindness—to take action that is necessary for *me* to do, because it is only *mine* to take—action that by deferral slides toward cruelty.

And action that, though necessary, can still feel regrettable. Because without regret, we have failed to imagine other, preferable turns of event. We have failed to leave room for the openness of what might be. We have settled for our own failure of imagination.

Regret is nothing to be sorry about. It's a sign that responsibility has been—and continues to be—borne. All that could be done was done. And when there was nothing else to be done, the last doing. Standing with hands open, the end of something dripping from my fingertips. Goodnight, sweet ones, with love on your lips and longing in your eyes.

303

The labyrinth entrance is oriented to the east, the direction of sunrise. I enter with no agenda. Troubles on my mind will make themselves heard, chattering until worn out and still. Sometimes I look down at the stones, their lichen universes, and the violets that hug them for warmth. Sometimes I look up to catch what sits beyond the labyrinth—young mountains to the west, old mountains to the east, a stand of birch trees to the south, and to the north a tree swing and the path back to my bed. By the time I exit (again, to the direction of sunrise) some thought or feeling may have floated up that I could never have predicted or named. Serendipity. A flicker of grace.

Labyrinths have been constructed and walked for ritual and religious reasons for millennia. Some people walk as meditation or as a charm for luck. *Help me win the lottery*, one note pleaded, left by someone needing a leg up. And as the slogan goes, you can't win if you don't enter.

304

I call the wise friend who advised me at the start of this sojourn. He was right about everything. I tell him I'm looking forward to getting back to my life. He tells me he's not sure *uhhh* he knows a story *hmmm* maybe a Zen teaching? Anyway, he says,

A young monk on the shore of a river shouts to an old monk on the other side of the river, "Hey, Master! How do I get to the other side?"

And the old monk shouts back, "What do you mean? You *are* on the other side!"

Acknowledgments

Particular thanks to

Dave Anolik, Ed Baggett LPN CHPLN, Bill & Nancy Branch,
Caron Christopherson, Molly Fiedler, Hattie Fletcher,
Alina Goman and family, Marcus Daly (Bitterroot Health)
Hospice Care, Kelly McElderry, David Markette, Helmut Meyer,
Michelle Meyer LMSW, Dany Naierman, Dr. Dean Solomon,
Tony Tharae, Tracey Turek, Les Woldstad

In memory of

Howard Liebhaber (1960-1992)
Florence Branch (1909-2010)
Janice Lee Porter (1953-2013)
Ailana Denison (1942-2014)
Patty Meyer (1948-2015)
Adele Branch (1931-2020)
Anna Storkson (1969-2021)
Harold Branch (1929-2021)
James Christopherson (1927-2021)
Lady (2003-2021)